LAUGH, CRY, AND BE INSPIRED
A TRUE STORY OF LO

I'll See You in the

Morning

*Where Do You Turn When the
Miracle Doesn't Come*

To Janeie
God Bless
Louise Flanders
Phil 1:12 NKJV

Louise D. Flanders

CONTENTS

Dedication

I'll See You in the Morning is dedicated first and foremost to my Lord and Savior Jesus Christ. My prayer has always been "that the things which have happened to me have actually turned out for the furtherance of the gospel" (Philippians 1:12). May Christ be glorified.

I also dedicate this book to Johnny, my kind, patient husband of 47 years. I can't imagine walking the path God has led us down with anyone other than you. We are a team. Thank you for believing in me when I didn't believe in myself, for encouraging me to put our story on paper, for being the spiritual leader in our home, and for never wavering in your faith in God. You are my encourager, my spiritual mentor, and my best friend.

Acknowledgements

I owe a huge debt of gratitude to my prayer team who faithfully asked God to bless my writing and who offered me ongoing encouragement and support. Thanks to: Glenn and JoAnn Birdwell, Larry and Wanda Cooley, Roger and Nancy Hines, Gloria James, Pam Kelsey, Phyllis Morris, Tom and Marty Parker, Wendy Porbandarwala, Faye Ross, Marsha Slagle, Mary Strayton, Gil and Joyce Wallace, and Kevin and Jamie Wallace,

I quickly realized when I first began writing *I'll See You in the Morning* that I needed help. I was thrilled to discover that a Christian writer's group met nearby. Christian Authors Guild gave me invaluable guidance in all aspects of writing, editing, and publishing. I continue to be an active member in this wonderful organization and am so thankful for the support they offer to Christian authors.

Thank you to Diana Baker, former editor of "Christian Living" magazine, for painstakingly editing *I'll See You in the Morning* several times. You rescued me from many overlooked grammar and punctuation errors. Thank you also for your sweet encouragement.

Thank you to our precious daughter Jamie, son-in-law Kevin, and grandchildren Will and Sydney for your ongoing support and help with Jonathan's care. Your love for Jonathan matches our own and his love for you is unsurpassed.

We will always be grateful to the members of our church, Roswell Street Baptist Church, and especially our Sunday school class, for the way they love Jonathan, pray for our family, and encourage and support us. You will hear God say, "Well done," someday for using your gifts for His glory.

And last but not least, thank you to my husband, Johnny. Without your computer skills, encouragement, and gentle prodding *I'll See You in the Morning* would never have been published.

.

Chapter 1

Early Signs

My heart pounded as I stared at our son, Jonathan, and listened to the constant hum of the enormous machines that occupied most of his room. He lay in the intensive care unit attached to a ventilator, a heart monitor, and a feeding machine. Multiple tubes of varying sizes and shapes snaked around the room, consuming practically every square inch. Pale and swollen, he lay perfectly still. His eyes remained closed, and his eyelids glistened with thick layers of protective gel. Curled in a fetal position, his small body bore little resemblance to my vivacious, cheerful, happy-go-lucky son. Today, January 11, 1983, was his seventh birthday, yet there would be no celebration. Jonathan's mind and body lay dormant, trapped in a deep coma.

I had never felt such dark despair. Tears spilled down my face and dampened my clothes. I kept thinking about our happy, energetic little boy and wondering how this could have happened. It was impossible to conceive that only eighteen months prior to this day our family had been experiencing the height of fun and happiness.

Disney World! Eight blissful days of rushing to grab a place in line, standing for hours in the unrelenting Florida sun, sweating from every crevice, all for the sheer thrill of experiencing three gut-wrenching minutes on a terrifying roller coaster. What could be more fun?

In August 1981 my husband, Johnny, and I both worked for the same company in Atlanta, Georgia, and we had saved for almost a year to take Jonathan, five years old at the time, and Jamie, his twelve-year-old sister, to Disney World. We had taken advantage of a comprehensive package that included everything from breakfast with Mickey Mouse and Donald Duck to a behind-the-scenes tour for Jamie that explained all the inner workings of Disney World.

Jonathan raced from ride to ride, pausing occasionally to grab a bear hug from Mickey, Donald, or Pluto. While Johnny and Jamie hurried off to experience anything that dipped, plunged, or hurled its victims at lightning speeds, Jonathan and I spent our days in Fantasyland twirling around in teacups and floating down a make-believe river while belting out "It's a Small World" at the top of our lungs. We had ridden Mr. Toad's Wild Ride so many times that I frantically searched for alternate routes around it to avoid having to ride it again.

At the close of each day, we fought our way back to Main Street to wrestle a spot along the curb for a prime view of the Electric Parade. The captivating music resonated in our heads long after we returned home. The crowning event of each day, however, was the grand fireworks extravaganza. Never had we seen anything so magnificent. Jonathan squealed with delight at each brilliant, colorful picture displayed in the sky.

Only one little problem emerged that threatened to spoil our perfect week. Jonathan had begun to notice a small amount of bleeding when he went to the bathroom. Even though he had always been small for his age, he had been healthy and had had a normal appetite, so we weren't overly concerned. We decided to make an appointment with his pediatrician as soon as we returned home, then we shoved it to the back of our minds for the rest of our vacation.

We all traipsed down to the lobby of our hotel when it came time to check out on Saturday, weighted down with suitcases, tote bags, and Disney souvenirs. Jamie and Jonathan's faces epitomized gloom and despair. Overcome with sorrow at having to leave Disney World, Jonathan suddenly burst into tears—loud blubbering that captured the attention of everyone in sight. As any good parent would have done, we promised him a return trip, candy, toys, a visit from Santa in September—anything to calm him down.

We spent the night with Johnny's parents in South Georgia on the way home. Worry fought its way into my mind and dominated my thinking. Jonathan's condition had worsened. The bleeding had become much more severe. With the euphoria of the trip beginning to fade, I felt desperate to return home and see his doctor.

Before our trip to Disney World, our lives had been busy and often hectic. Johnny and I had met and had fallen in love at East Texas Baptist University in Marshall, Texas. We married in 1966 when we were only half-way through college. My heart's desire had always been to be a nurse; however, East Texas Baptist University did not offer a nursing program at that time. I decided to major in sociology instead. Little did I know how God would use that love for medicine and nursing at a crucial time in our lives. Johnny, a ministerial student, had continued daily to seek direction from God concerning our future.

After graduating college in 1968, we packed all our meager belongings in our car and headed to Southwestern Seminary in Fort Worth, Texas. After three months and much prayer, we determined that full-time ministry was not the direction in which God was leading us. We knew beyond any doubt what God did *not* want us to do; unfortunately, we didn't have a clue what He *did* want us to do. Without any warning, we found ourselves in a precarious situation—Johnny with no direction and no job and me six months pregnant.

Thankfully, God always shows up at exactly the right moment. Johnny received a phone call from a former business manager asking him to consider a job in Atlanta, Georgia. He readily accepted; and once again, we loaded all our earthly possessions into our car and a U-Haul trailer and headed east.

I had lived in Texas almost all my life, but reluctantly agreed to leave my beloved state. Johnny, a thoroughbred Georgian, filled my mind with visions of tall pines, rolling hills, cool gentle breezes, and sweet southern tea. The sweet tea won me over. We arrived in Atlanta on a cold December day in 1968, along with my parents who had followed close behind us to help their pregnant daughter move and unpack.

We had barely settled in when our daughter, Jamie, arrived in the wee hours of the morning on March 8, 1969. By that time, Johnny had begun a promising career as a computer programmer with a large utility company in Atlanta; and I had begun to delight in my role as a full-time mom. In 1973 I began working at the same company where Johnny worked, and we purchased our first home in Marietta, Georgia, a suburb on the north side of Atlanta.

In January 1976 after seven years of being an only child, Jamie finally had a baby brother. Jonathan made his debut into this world kicking and screaming and full of energy. From day one, he could not have been more different from Jamie. She was quiet, calm, easy to discipline, and eager to please. She loved nothing better than reading, and she thrived on learning. We quickly realized that Jonathan's personality produced opposite traits. A born extrovert, bursting with personality and energy, he never met a stranger. He talked non-stop and came out of the womb strong-willed, loving the spotlight, and determined about everything.

Once when he was around four years of age, he disobeyed, and Johnny sent him to his room to reflect on his errant ways. Johnny said very firmly, "Jonathan, do not step your foot out of your room until I say that you can come out." Before Johnny completed the sentence, Jonathan locked eyes with Johnny and deliberately stuck his little foot just barely over the threshold in an act of defiance. If he wanted to do something badly enough, no punishment deterred him. We knew from the start we were in for an interesting ride. We saw in the years that followed that his strong-willed personality, though often difficult to mold, was actually a gift from God that kept him from giving up when the odds were stacked against him.

A few weeks before our trip to Disney World, I experienced something I had never experienced before. An overwhelming sense of depression threatened to engulf me. It seemed to come out of nowhere. Working full-time and managing a household and two children created a hectic and exhausting schedule, but one that I normally handled with ease. This dark oppressive mood frightened me. After several weeks of crying almost incessantly, I made a decision. I asked Johnny one evening if he would take the children somewhere—anywhere—so that I could have some time alone.

Even before I heard the car drive away, the tears began to flow—agonizing, heartrending sobs that I couldn't understand or control. I had given my heart and my life to Christ at eight years of age and I was no stranger to prayer. I knew first-hand that prayer, the ability to communicate with God and Him with us, was one of the greatest gifts God had given to us. I slipped to my knees and cried out to Him in desperation. I begged Him to lift this spirit of oppression and despondency from my life. I recommitted my life completely to Him and asked Him to use my life in any way that would please Him.

I don't know how many hours I remained in that room talking with God, but when I came out, I experienced a new spirit of joy and expectancy. I knew beyond any shadow of a doubt that something life-changing was about to take place. I had no way of knowing what the future held for us, but I sensed a renewed excitement and joy about my relationship with the Lord and a confidence that whatever happened, He would carry us through. I had no idea that He had used that experience to draw me close to Him and to prepare my heart for what lay ahead. I had no way of knowing that within a matter of weeks our lives would change forever.

Chapter 2

Medical Diagnosis

Following our trip to Disney World, we made an appointment the first week in September with Jonathan's pediatrician. We were relieved that he didn't consider Jonathan's condition serious, but probably the result of a small tear or fissure. He prescribed some medication and told us to call if he was not better within a week. Our relief was short-lived. In just a matter of days, his condition worsened considerably.

I attempted to remain calm for Jonathan's sake, but I felt a growing sense of anxiety in the pit of my stomach. What could possibly be causing the bleeding? I plundered through my crowded bookshelves until I located my layman's medical encyclopedia. I began searching for any possible answer, all the while praying that Jonathan didn't have a life-threatening condition.

Neither Johnny nor I wanted to verbalize our greatest fear. If we refused to say the word "cancer" aloud, maybe, just maybe, it would be something else.

Jonathan's pediatrician gave us the names of the only two pediatric gastroenterologists in Atlanta at that time; one located at Emory University Hospital, a long drive from where we lived; the other at Scottish Rite Hospital (SRH) within a mile of where Johnny and I worked. We immediately contacted the doctor at Scottish Rite.

We entered his office the day of our appointment with mixed emotions—relief to receive a diagnosis—and fear of what that diagnosis would be. Jonathan appeared to be the only one totally relaxed and completely unconcerned. He sat cross-legged in the floor of the waiting room playing and chatting with the other children as we waited for the nurse to call his name.

We had not been waiting long when suddenly the door opened and a short, middle-aged man entered the waiting room, sat down cross-legged on the floor next to Jonathan and extended his right hand. "Hi. You must be Jonathan. Would you like some M and M's?" he asked. The two of them sat on the floor like life-long friends discussing the merits of M & M's versus Reese's Pieces and other similar candies and arguing about which color was the most delectable. That unorthodox meeting marked the beginning of a very long relationship between doctor and patient.

The gastroenterologist assured us that a number of conditions could cause Jonathan's hemorrhaging and the best approach involved running a series of tests until he obtained an accurate diagnosis. Thankfully, he didn't waste any time getting started. He scheduled the first test, a colonoscopy, the next week at the hospital. We explained to Jonathan that he would be having a medical test but that he would be asleep the entire time. As the day approached, we could sense a growing anxiety. Jonathan seemed scared for the first time. We had tried to downplay his illness so as not to frighten him, but he grew quieter and more subdued as the day of his procedure drew near. It became increasingly difficult to hide our anxiety. I couldn't focus on anything else. One minute I experienced God's peace and comfort, and the next minute fear threatened to suffocate me.

On the day of his test, we arrived at the hospital early, and a nurse ushered us into a curtained cubicle to change Jonathan's clothes. She recited instructions in a rote tone of voice, suggesting many years of repeating the same sentences. "He needs to put on this gown with it open in the back, and place all of his clothes and shoes in this bag."

"I have to wear a gown!" Jonathan's giggles broke the tension as I slid the child-sized garment covered with miniature cars over his arms and tied the strings in the back. The smile quickly faded, however, when the nurse returned with a handful of needles to start an IV. His big velvety brown eyes turned to pools of liquid as she probed for a "good" vein. She quickly injected the sedating medication, and his eyelids gradually closed. I stopped just short of asking her to sedate me also.

To our surprise, the doctor called us back and allowed us to see what he viewed through the scope. Since we had no way to interpret what appeared on the screen, the doctor provided an explanation: Jonathan did not have cancer, but ulcers covered his entire colon. Shock registered on the doctor's face. "I have never seen ulcerative colitis this severe in a five-year-old child," he whispered. He gathered biopsy samples of the intestinal lining that later confirmed the diagnosis.

We were stunned! We were greatly relieved that Jonathan didn't have cancer, but we knew nothing about ulcerative colitis. Where in the world had it come from? How had he gotten it? Was it curable? Questions bombarded our minds. We had never known anyone with that disease except senior citizens. How could our little five-year-old son have gotten it? Armed with pamphlets, prescriptions, and appointments for more tests, we returned home determined to find a cure.

I began to research everything I could get my hands on about ulcerative colitis. What I discovered alarmed and frightened me. Ulcers and inflammation in the colon characterized the disease, but it was thankfully, confined to the colon. The severity of the disease could vary. Unfortunately, Jonathan's disease affected his entire colon. The cause of ulcerative colitis remained a mystery (it is still unknown today), but doctors suspected a bacteria or virus could possibly trigger a deficiency in the immune system of the large bowel. According to Jonathan's doctor, his disease resembled an autoimmune disease, in that his body appeared to be rejecting his colon. When I read that ulcerative colitis could also run in families, I remembered that years before, my mother had experienced a very mild case of the disease. Jonathan's doctor also informed us that the risk of colon cancer increased greatly when a person had ulcerative colitis for eight to ten years. Medications and treatments were available, and we were anxious to get started.

Appointments, lab work, tests, tests, and more tests filled our calendar in the following weeks. Jonathan accused the lab technicians of turning him into a pincushion.

In 1981 many physicians felt the disease stemmed from emotional stress. His doctor questioned Johnny and me about Jonathan's personal life. Was he a happy child? Had he recently experienced any trauma such as the loss of a grandparent or a much-loved pet? We assured his doctor that Jonathan had always been happy and cheerful. God had blessed him with a joyful spirit even at five years of age. Even though abdominal pain had become his constant companion, he rarely complained. Whatever the cause, we were positive it did not stem from stress.

In spite of the doctor visits and continuing evidence of Jonathan's illness, we attempted to keep his life as normal as possible. Before he became ill, he had attended a kindergarten program near where we worked. On days that he felt well enough, we allowed him to continue to attend, but his teachers were becoming understandably nervous about his medical condition. We explained that ulcerative colitis was not contagious, and that it was important psychologically for him to maintain his normal routine when possible.

Although Jonathan daily consumed multiple medications designed to heal his diseased colon, on October 6, 1981, he took a decided turn for the worse. By that time he was having over twenty bowel movements a day and the commode was always full of blood. However, on that day when he awoke, his stomach appeared large and distended and his face ashen. We rushed him to the doctor's office and frantically called friends from church to pray for him. The doctor took one look at him and wrote orders to admit him to the hospital immediately. The seriousness of the situation began to sink in when the doctor denied my request to first go home and pack his pajamas and toothbrush. His lab work revealed that his blood count, because of all his hemorrhaging, had dropped dangerously low.

Johnny left work immediately and met us at the hospital. After we completed reams of paper work, a semi-private room finally became available for Jonathan. Thankfully, the other bed remained unoccupied giving us a measure of privacy. Jonathan seemed content to curl up under the covers and lapse into sleep.

Since we had no idea how long he would be in the hospital, I insisted that Johnny return to work. He reluctantly agreed and promised to return with Jamie after work. While Jonathan slept and I waited for the nurse to come, my mind whirled in a thousand directions. Neither of our children had ever spent time in the hospital, and my emotions bordered on hysteria. I tried concentrating on the primary-colored animals on the curtains. When the red elephants and blue giraffes failed to calm my shattered nerves, I opened the blinds and tried to focus on the activities outside the window. I had never felt so helpless. I bowed my head and prayed for God's peace. I begged Him to restore Jonathan's health and pleaded with Him not to let Jonathan die from this strange disease.

I heard the rustling of the nurse's uniform and the rapid rise and fall of her footsteps long before she appeared in Jonathan's room. She entered dragging an IV pole behind her with miles of plastic tubing attached to it. Jonathan's eyes gradually opened, and he squinted cautiously at the nurse. He instantly became wide-awake, his eyes huge in his small face. I followed his gaze and understood his fear. She clutched in her right hand the dreaded needles he had come to recognize, and that could only mean one thing. The doctor had ordered a blood transfusion immediately because of his low blood count. She located a "good" vein almost immediately, and we were thankful for her competence.

Much to Jonathan's dismay, the doctor also placed him on a liquid diet in an attempt to "rest" his colon and allow it to heal. Limiting fresh fruits and vegetables often helps control mild cases of ulcerative colitis by reducing irritation to the large bowel. Because of the severity of his disease, however, his doctor restricted him to liquids only. Knowing he could not eat only made him focus on food even more. He was definitely my child. Pizza, hamburgers, hot dogs, and macaroni and cheese—all his favorite foods—completely occupied his mind.

Normally too busy to sit still for long, his fear became almost visible as he crawled into my lap for comfort. I gathered him in my arms trying to be careful of his transfusion tubes and drew comfort from being able to hold him close. While the dark red solution snaked its way through the tubes and into his little body, he squirmed to nestle his head against my shoulder. Unfortunately, we both forgot about his IV tubing. Suddenly the transfusion line popped loose! The plastic tube jerked around, flying wildly out of control. Blood spurted everywhere—all over the bed, Jonathan, and me. Peals of laughter erupted from Jonathan. He thought it was hilarious. Even though I didn't think it was quite as comical as he did, our shared laughter helped the tension melt away.

Late that afternoon we had our first visitor. My supervisor dropped by after work to check on Jonathan and to visit with us, his face almost completely hidden behind several brightly colored helium balloons attached to a huge basket. He had filled the basket with numerous individually wrapped toys, one for each day that Jonathan was in the hospital. It would necessitate some restraint for Jonathan to open only one a day, but it would give him something to focus on and look forward to other than his illness. My supervisor also gave me a gift, the gift of time. Because I had accumulated the maximum amount of sick leave possible, he informed me that I could use that time to stay with Jonathan until he was well. Neither of us had any idea that day that I would deplete all of my sick leave long before Jonathan's health returned.

Johnny and Jamie arrived shortly after my supervisor left, and we began a routine that would last many days. I arrived at the hospital each morning in time for Johnny to leave for work. I stayed all day Monday through Friday. Johnny left work at 5:00 p.m., picked Jamie up from an after-school program, and then drove to the hospital. Johnny spent Sunday through Thursday nights at the hospital, attempting to sleep on the bed-want-a-be (the hospital chair) until someone graciously loaned us a cot. Each morning he showered, shaved, and dressed for work at the hospital. Each weekend we switched schedules. I spent Friday and Saturday nights at the hospital, and stayed home Saturday during the day to catch-up on laundry, grocery shopping, and housework. Jamie and I were also able to spend some desperately needed quality time together each Saturday.

Scottish Rite had only semi-private rooms at that time, and Jonathan's first roommate was a precious little nine-year-old boy from Columbia, South America. An American family had adopted him at four years of age. Because he had developed polio at a young age, one of his legs remained underdeveloped and shorter than the other leg. He had spent a considerable amount of time at Scottish Rite undergoing numerous surgeries to lengthen his leg. He knew all the nurses and the inner workings of the hospital. He and Jonathan became fast friends. The two of them spent hours planning an elaborate party they intended to host at McDonald's, feasting on their favorite cuisine, when they were both well.

By the tenth day of Jonathan's hospital stay, we began to see a slight improvement in his condition. He was still on a liquid diet and small doses of prednisone to heal the inflammation in his colon. The prednisone had some side effects that were undesirable, but it did seem to be working. One unusual side effect involved strange tingling sensations in his arms and legs. I blamed the medicine when he announced one day that his leg felt "frisky."

Chapter 3

Ambulance Ride, Television Debut, and More Delays

Ten days evolved into three weeks before Jonathan came home from the hospital. He was on large doses of prednisone medication and on a very restricted diet that did not include his longed-for pizza and hamburgers. I returned to work and Jonathan went back to kindergarten. It felt wonderful to regain some semblance of our normal routine.

Unfortunately, it was not to last. After an incredibly short three weeks, he began to hemorrhage again, and we found ourselves back at Scottish Rite Hospital. We began another round of blood transfusions, liquid diets, and even larger doses of medication. In addition to the oral prednisone medication he had been taking for inflammation, he now also required IV hydrocortisone. It seemed as though he had never left the hospital.

It was becoming more and more difficult emotionally to see him continually being stuck with needles, unable to eat any solid foods, and never able to run and play with his friends. Jonathan's IV malfunctioned frequently. We all dreaded those times. The nurse would haul him off to the treatment room and stick him with needles repeatedly until a good vein could be located. Patients two floors away heard his cries every time that happened. Finally, his doctor suggested we put in a subclavian catheter, which provided a more permanent solution and eliminated the need to constantly probe for good veins. Inserting the catheter was a surgical procedure requiring a pediatric surgeon at Scottish Rite Hospital to join our growing team of doctors. According to the hospital grapevine, he was the best of the best.

Word began to spread throughout our church and neighborhood that Jonathan was very sick. Stacks of cards and gifts arrived daily. Savory casseroles and mouth-watering desserts prepared by members of our Sunday school class arrived at our hospital room several times a week. Nothing in the world compares to a group of Christian women committed to demonstrating God's love to those in need. They wrote the manual on caring for people. Of course, Jonathan loved all the gifts and attention, and Johnny, Jamie, and I loved all the delicious food.

My friend, Emelynn, and I were co-workers who spent our days writing customer accounting procedures for several utility companies. Emelynn had previously taught elementary school for several years and she was a born teacher. She began coming to the hospital frequently during her lunch hour or after work, and Jonathan fell in love with her. They worked puzzles together and made crafts. Their laughter floated up and down the hospital corridors. It was hard to tell which of them was having the most fun. She always came armed with lots of interesting books, and they would read together for hours. Often Emelynn stayed with Jonathan while Johnny, Jamie, and I ate dinner together in the cafeteria. We made it a rule never to eat in front of Jonathan because solid foods were still on his forbidden list. Emelynn's presence allowed the three of us a semblance of family time together without having to worry about leaving Jonathan unattended.

Gradually the air outdoors turned chilly. The trees outside our window painted the landscape with glorious displays of red, orange, and yellow leaves like a colorful parade marching by. It was my favorite time of the year, but I could view it only from the confines of Jonathan's hospital window.

Thanksgiving 1981 found us still imprisoned behind the hospital walls. On December 2 we were finally able once more to stop the progression of the disease and return home. We spotted the "WELCOME HOME" sign covering most of our front door long before we pulled into the driveway. The neighborhood children had devoted a lot of time to working on the sign to let Jonathan know how much they missed him.

Jonathan was taking lots of medication and was limited to a restricted diet, but we were determined to take our focus off his illness and concentrate instead on the upcoming Christmas season. He and Jamie spent many hours pouring over catalogs and creating lengthy Christmas lists while I frantically raced through department stores trying to play "catch-up."

Between hospital stays, we tried to keep our lives and schedules as normal as possible. One particular Wednesday night, we were attending a prayer service together at our church. Because of Jonathan's lack of stamina, we had positioned ourselves near the rear of the church. When it came time for prayer requests the pastor said, "We are so pleased that Jonathan Flanders and his family could join us this evening. As most of you know, Jonathan has been in and out of the hospital for several months, and we are still praying for his total healing. Jonathan, can you tell us how many days you have spent at Scottish Rite Hospital?" Relishing all the attention lavished on him, Jonathan climbed up on the church pew so everyone could see him and shouted as loudly as he could in a booming voice, "Way too many!" No one ever accused him of being shy.

My entire family—two brothers, one sister, and their families—had planned to gather at my parents' home in Columbia, Mississippi to celebrate Christmas. Regardless of where we each lived, at Christmastime we all looked forward to the pilgrimage home to celebrate Christmas together.

They were all aware that Jonathan had been very ill, and we knew they had been praying for his recovery, but the physical changes he had undergone shocked everyone. He had always been small for his age, even slightly underweight, but the enormous amounts of prednisone medication he had consumed trying to keep his disease at bay had taken a toll. The medicine had given him a colossal appetite and had caused him to retain fluid. He was almost as wide as he was tall, and his stamina was practically zero.

I have never been more proud of my family. I knew they were shocked at his appearance, but there was no mention of it whatsoever. Even his cousins treated him as though he had never been sick a day in his life.

As we gathered around the piano to sing the cherished Christmas carols and read the precious story of Christ's birth from Daddy's Bible, I could only pray that the new year would bring healing to our son.

The fireworks and festivities that welcomed 1982 were still fresh on our minds when Jonathan's sixth birthday rolled around on January 11. Physically weakened from the disease and from the medications his body required to fight the disease, we limited the celebration to a small party at home with a few of his close friends.

By February the ulcerative colitis had returned with a vengeance. His doctors agreed it was time to consider surgically removing his diseased colon. He could no longer continue to take large doses of the cortisone medication.

At his doctors' recommendation, we consulted the pediatric gastroenterologist at Emory University Hospital for a second opinion. He was in complete agreement and was actually amazed that Jonathan had managed to avoid the surgery that long. We were all so exhausted physically and emotionally from our six-month medical ordeal that we were ready to do whatever it took to see him restored to health.

Before we entered the hospital again, I knew I had to make a decision about my job. I had taken all of my accumulated sick leave and as much personal leave without pay as I was allowed. Even though I had worked for the same company for over ten years, Jonathan's health had to be my first priority. Financially, Johnny and I needed my income, especially with the medical bills mounting daily, but we both knew it was time for me to resign and trust God with our needs. Philippians 4:19 states, "My God shall supply all your need according to His riches in glory by Christ Jesus." We thanked God for that promise and trusted Him to take care of our financial needs. It was a relief to turn in my resignation and no longer feel torn between my son and my job.

Jonathan reentered the hospital on February 16. We were well aware that it would not be a short stay. We knew it would take several weeks for his body to heal sufficiently for him to be able to undergo surgery. Amazingly, Jonathan's attitude up until then had been positive and optimistic. This time, however, he hated the thought of going back to the hospital, and nobody could blame him. He longed to be able to go back to church and kindergarten and to play with his friends. We were all clinging to the hope that his surgery would provide healing, and we would be able to return to our normal lifestyle.

On February 25 his gastro doctor performed a sigmoidoscopy and a biopsy to see if he was ready for surgery. Removing his colon meant it would be necessary for him to have an ileostomy bag for at least a few months. The surgeon would create a pouch and a valve from the lower end of the small intestine (the ileum). The valve would be connected to an opening (stoma) in the skin of the lower abdomen. That would allow the bowel fluid to empty into the ileostomy bag. In order to close off his ileostomy when the time came, a small section of his colon, about twelve-inches long, would need to remain intact near the rectal area.

The disease had always attacked the inner lining of Jonathan's colon. The doctors hoped during his surgery to remove that inner lining from the twelve-inch section. However, following the sigmoidoscopy and the biopsy, both doctors agreed there was still too much inflammation present to proceed safely with surgery. They were almost as frustrated as we were with the tenacity of Jonathan's disease and the inability to conquer it. His surgeon even took the initiative to contact the surgeon who had originally pioneered that particular surgical procedure just to ensure that he was doing everything possible to bring about a cure.

The nurses and staff at the hospital were rapidly becoming our extended family. Marsha and Lisel were definite favorites. Pretty, young, and single, Marsha with her warm personality drew people like a magnet. Her strong faith in Christ provided a common bond, and we quickly became friends. Married to a minister whom we had known for several years, Lisel, like Marsha, radiated beauty inside and out. Her contagious smile matched her sweet, gentle personality. Jonathan managed to wrap both nurses around his little finger in no time.

One day a woman we had never met walked into Jonathan's room. She introduced herself as Jane, the "ostomy" therapist. She had come to answer our questions and prepare Jonathan for having an ileostomy bag following surgery. *How in the world do you prepare a six-year-old child for something like an ostomy bag?* I wondered! I had never even seen an ostomy bag, and quite frankly, I didn't even know anyone who had one. It wasn't exactly something people discussed at parties. I was very worried about how Jonathan would adapt to the idea.

The therapist showed us different types of bags and talked to Jonathan about the importance of chewing his food well, not swallowing any gum, cutting raisins in half so they wouldn't swell and block the flow—blah, blah, blah, blah, blah! A migraine slowly began to work its way from the back of my head to the front just listening to her spiel. *Poor Jonathan. What kind of reaction must he be having?* I wondered. I was afraid to look at him.

When the therapist asked Jonathan if he had any questions, I stole a glance his way and held my breath. (We never knew what would come out of his mouth.) "Yes, I do," he replied emphatically. "Can I eat pizza and hamburgers when I get this bag?"

"Of course. If you chew your food well, you will be able to eat almost anything you want," she said.

"Then what are we waiting for?" he replied. "Let's have the surgery so I can have something good to eat!" Who would have guessed?

I entered his room early on March 2 and knew immediately something was wrong. Johnny related that Jonathan had been having difficulty breathing and was obviously not feeling well. Jonathan looked completely miserable. Marsha was his nurse for the morning, and she had already paged his doctor, who arrived within minutes. He quickly strapped an oxygen mask around Jonathan's mouth and nostrils and wheeled him down to x-ray.

Somehow, his subclavian catheter had dislodged overnight routing all of his IV fluids into his lungs. His doctor attempted to reposition the catheter, but after several failed attempts, he had to remove the line entirely. A nurse inserted an IV on his hand, but removing the fluid from Jonathan's lungs turned the situation into an emergency. The doctor allowed me to stay with Jonathan, explaining what they were going to do and instructing me to let him know if I felt queasy. Jonathan sat on the edge of the examination table facing me. He placed his head on my shoulder while the doctor numbed an area of his back. My eyes nearly fell out of their sockets when I saw the needle. It looked like an extremely long ice pick. I didn't know they made needles that long. I said a quick silent prayer of thanks that Jonathan was facing me and could not see it.

They drew out a substantial amount of fluid and then sent him back to x-ray. He still had a small amount of fluid in the bottom of both lungs, and his right lung had collapsed. A respiratory therapist began working with him to expand his lungs, and he began taking antibiotics to prevent infection. We were beginning to breathe a little easier, but over the following days, he began to run a fever and to cough continuously. Two days after the catheter dislodged, his left arm turned blue and began to swell and cause pain. He had developed a blood clot at the site of the previous catheter. That was obviously a cause for alarm. If the clot traveled to his heart or lungs, it could be fatal. Suddenly, the urgency of the impending surgery took a back seat to the impending crisis.

We called our pastor and members of our Sunday school class and asked them to pray. The following day his doctor ordered an electrocardiogram (EKG) and a lung scan to make sure the clot had not moved. The lung scan required a trip across the street to another hospital. The hospital sent an ambulance and the driver gently lifted Jonathan onto a stretcher and slid him into the back.

The assistant director of nursing accompanied Jonathan and gave me permission to ride in the back with him. Johnny arranged to meet us at the hospital.

Worry about Jonathan's medical condition pushed every other thought from my mind. Before the ambulance drove away, Jonathan lifted his head and said he needed to ask the ambulance driver a question. I listened intently, afraid that he was experiencing new symptoms. My fears were definitely unfounded.

"Could you please turn on the siren? I've never ridden in an ambulance before, and I want to hear the siren." He wanted to experience that ride to the fullest. The driver loved it. He flashed on the overhead lights, activated the siren, and we went roaring across the street at top speed, stopping traffic in all directions. It was exhilarating!

Jonathan's test took about two-and-a-half hours. When it was over, the driver loaded him back in the ambulance, turned on the flashing lights, reactivated the sirens, and zoomed back across the street. It was better than any medication the doctor could have prescribed.

Jonathan's doctor brought good news later that day. The clot had not traveled to his lungs. Since it had not moved within twenty-four hours, the likelihood that it would travel was remote. There was still fluid in his lungs, but hopefully with respiratory therapy that would improve.

That evening we had a small celebration. A couple of weeks earlier a local television crew had taped a segment at Scottish Rite for a show called PM Magazine. A short portion of the show featured none other than Jonathan. Not only did Jonathan experience his first ambulance ride that day, but he also made his television debut. We all crowded around his tiny hospital television and reveled in his five minutes of fame.

My parents arrived from Mississippi that evening to give us a much-needed break and to celebrate Jamie's thirteenth birthday. They insisted we stay away from the hospital all weekend and let them spend time with Jonathan. They didn't have to twist our arms.

We spent Saturday purchasing birthday gifts and planning a "mini" party for Jamie, complete with a Smurf cake made by a friend. It is easy to become so absorbed with a critically ill child that other children feel neglected. Jamie had been a trooper, but we didn't want to lose sight of the fact that Jonathan's ongoing medical problems prevented any hope of a normal lifestyle. Nothing about our lives was "normal."

The following week Jonathan improved in every way, and everything looked positive for surgery on March 16. As much as we all dreaded it, we were ready to put it behind us and reclaim our lives.

Once again, trouble reared its ugly head. Saturday morning we were all in Jonathan's room taking advantage of some family time together when he began coughing and having breathing difficulties again. As soon as we notified his nurse, doctors, nurses, x-ray equipment, and respiratory technicians flooded his room. For some reason, fluid was once again filling his lungs. His surgeon drew out more fluid from his lungs and sent it to the lab. In spite of the fact that it was Saturday and his doctor was obviously exhausted from having been in emergency surgery all day, he returned at 10:30 that evening to check on Jonathan. His concern was not just from a medical standpoint. It was apparent that he genuinely cared deeply for Jonathan—and the feeling was mutual. He broke the dreaded news that there was no way we could consider surgery on the sixteenth in light of his current lung problems.

We had been at Scottish Rite "that stay" for a month, and we still didn't have a date for surgery. I could feel despondency settling deep within my soul. That night sleep would not come. I tossed and turned, worried about whether Jonathan would ever be well enough for surgery. I knew he could not live much longer without the surgery, but I was terrified of the outcome. Finally, I got out of bed, got on my knees, and in the darkened room once again surrendered my fears for my only son to the One who knew the pain of seeing His only son suffer. I begged Him for a miracle—a miracle so powerful that surgery would not be necessary. And, if that wasn't God's plan, then I prayed for the surgery to be successful and for a complete, total healing.

The following week we were in the treatment room once again with a nurse desperately trying to locate a viable vein. Jonathan had perfected the art of praying aloud—really loud—when the nurse stuck him with a needle. On that particular day, he was beseeching all of heaven in a loud voice.

"O, God, please help them to stop sticking me with these awful needles. God, get me out of this place soon. God, when am I going to get to eat pizza and hamburgers again?" On and on he prayed, invoking the very throne of God as only a six-year-old can. Suddenly, he stopped praying and yelled to his doctor who had stepped in the room when he heard all the commotion, "Are you praying for me?"

With a restrained smile his doctor replied, "Yes, Jonathan. I'm praying for you."

To which Jonathan replied, "Well, could you please pray out loud? I can't hear you!"

Jesus said in Mark 10:15, "Whoever does not receive the kingdom of God as a little child will by no means enter it." I think Jonathan was a shoo-in!

Thankfully, the next week Jonathan's doctor was able to put in a more permanent central-line catheter that, we prayed, would prove to be more reliable. We were all grateful they could finally stopped poking him with needles.

Chapter 4

Spring Flowers and Ministering Angels

Jonathan's doctors rescheduled his surgery for April 6, and we asked everyone to pray that he would be well enough to go through with it.

By this time, the staff at Scottish Rite had practically adopted Jonathan as one of their own. They spoiled him outrageously. Even the housekeepers visited him on their breaks and daily showered him with toys from the hospital gift shop. The floor secretary nicknamed him "Mr. Personality" and placed a huge sign over the door to his room to make it official.

Outside Jonathan's hospital window, daffodils and tulips loudly screamed that spring had arrived. Small, immature, green leaves sprouted on the trees, and the grass had turned that beautiful shade of green that is only on display during spring's fashion show. Jonathan desperately wanted to break out of the confines of the hospital.

Emelynn had the perfect solution. She arrived at the hospital one beautiful Saturday morning lugging huge boxes of planting supplies. She brought a long plastic planting box, potting soil, seeds, fertilizer, and gardening tools. After exiling us from the room, she and Jonathan set to work. They carefully filled the planting box with soil, and then together their fingers became plows making deep furrows in the soil to house the future floral display. Tiny flower seeds of varying species filled the trenches. Painstakingly, they folded the soil over the seeds, hiding them from view. After watering and fertilizing, they stood back to admire their handiwork. Jonathan was quivering with excitement. The anticipation of the future floral oasis was exactly the diversion he needed.

We developed a new friend while we were awaiting surgery—a secret pal. Jonathan began almost daily receiving cards, stickers, books, toys and puzzles from his new mysterious friend. We spent hours speculating about the identity of this obscure benefactor. There was never a hint of a return address, and all notes were printed neatly and simply signed "your secret pal."

That phantom friend provided an air of mystery that enthralled Jonathan. He would lie in bed and try to guess who it could be. A year slipped by before we learned the identity of our elusive friend. A woman from our church had heard about Jonathan and had been praying for a way to encourage him. The idea of being his secret pal began to take shape. To the best of my knowledge, we had never met her before he became ill. She will always hold a special place in our hearts as one of God's "unsung heroes" who encouraged Jonathan and ministered to all of us.

Another unlikely friendship developed during that hospital stay. We were understandably becoming a constant drain on our company's health insurance because of Jonathan's lengthy illness. Even though we worked in Atlanta, our insurance company's headquarters was in Birmingham, Alabama. It was necessary for us to call the insurance company from time to time to explain and clarify Jonathan's medical claims. A young woman named Jessica was primarily responsible for handling Jonathan's copious claims. Though she had never met Jonathan personally, he began to emerge in her heart and mind as a very real person, a very sick little boy, and not just an insurance statistic. She decided to become his pen pal. She frequently sent cards and letters with assurances that she was praying for him daily.

Our church continued to minister to our family in the most practical ways. We had joined Roswell Street Baptist Church located in Marietta in 1973, shortly after moving to Marietta. I'll never forget our first visit and our decision to join that wonderful fellowship of believers. We had always loved the closeness and warmth of a small fellowship and had agreed that we would only visit small congregations. However, after visiting several small churches, we decided we would visit Roswell Street Baptist one time, but only once. They had a membership of over 3,000 at that time, not exactly the definition of a small church.

We arrived early and managed to find three empty seats next to each other. Long before the service began, the sanctuary filled to capacity. As we waited for the service to begin, the choir filed in energetically belting out "Victory in Jesus." They smiled and sang with great enthusiasm. We loved it. In fact, we loved everything about Roswell Street Baptist Church.

In spite of our desire for a small fellowship, we both knew this was our new church home. We joined the next Sunday. Only God could have known the overwhelming circumstances that would surround our family in the years to come. Only He could have known how He would use that church to meet so many needs in our lives. We joined in April 1973 and are still members there today.

Our Sunday school class attempted to provide meals on an ongoing basis, but because we seemed to have taken up permanent residence at Scottish Rite, they needed help. I'm sure we were wearing them out. I have no idea to this day how they organized and coordinated it, but different Sunday school classes all over the church began providing meals for us on a rotating basis. Whoever prepared the meal delivered it to the hospital so we could eat together as a family. If we had gone to x-ray or somewhere else within the hospital, whoever brought the meal frequently left it in Jonathan's room. We often had no idea who had prepared it. Members of our church brought meals about three times a week, and it was always enough for at least two days. On the rare occasions that I was able to attend church, invariably church members whom I had never met would introduce themselves, inquire about Jonathan, and share that they had prepared a meal for us. Total strangers ministering to our needs. I joked that I needed a t-shirt stating, "I'm Jonathan's mom!" Everyone in the church knew who he was even if they didn't know Johnny and me.

Though we appreciated everyone's help, it was extremely difficult to be on the receiving end. When Jesus said in Acts 20:35, "It is more blessed to give than to receive." He could have likewise said, "It is also *easier* to give than to receive!" On one particular occasion when I was feeling depressed about being such a burden to everyone, a friend gently reminded me that helping our family allowed our friends to serve God and utilize their spiritual gifts. And it was a tremendous help.

I practically lived at the hospital from early morning until nighttime every day, leaving no time at all to shop for groceries or prepare meals. When I arrived home each night, I wanted and needed to devote what little time I had to Jamie before falling exhausted into bed.

The Lord taught me a valuable lesson about serving others. I had always assumed that when you helped others it was simply a ministry to the family who needed help. And it definitely is that. There is, however, an often-overlooked aspect to giving to others: It is a witness to the rest of the world. Jesus said in Matthew 5:16, "Let your light so shine before men, that they may see your good works and glorify your Father in heaven." Everyone in the hospital was able to "see the good works" that our church family lavished on us, and it was a powerful witness to God's mercy and grace.

Often when we had more food than we could eat, we placed the leftovers in the nurses' station to share with them. On one particular occasion, we had lined the counter of the nurses' station with several platters of food. One of the doctors rounded the corner, spotted the food, and his face lit up at the prospect of a "home-cooked" meal. "Where did this come from?" No sooner were the words out of his mouth than he followed it with, "Oh, your church friends must have been here again today!"

Letters were beginning to pour in from pastors and friends from other churches—many from distant states—assuring us of their prayers for Jonathan. A friend of mine from high school, James Messer, whom I had not seen since graduation, served as a pastor in Mississippi. His entire congregation sent a letter expressing their concern and prayer support. Everyone who had attended a Wednesday night prayer service had signed it.

We taped every card and letter to the wall in Jonathan's room so he could look at each one and be encouraged. Often he would point to a favorite card and asked us to get it down for him to look at again. Eventually, his cards more than filled the entire space, and we had to begin rotating them.

Chapter 5

The Long-Awaited Surgery

As we inched closer to our surgery date, new problems cropped up. Jonathan began experiencing excruciating back pain, so severe he could not stand up without screaming in pain. An orthopedic doctor examined him and ordered x-rays. The heavy doses of prednisone and hydrocortisone he consumed daily had weakened his bones and had caused a hairline fracture in one of his vertebrae. The doctor placed him on total bed rest and ordered him to lie flat on his back until the fracture healed.

My heart ached for him. He had eaten nothing by mouth for almost two months, and now he couldn't even walk to the hospital playroom. To keep up his spirits, we transferred him to a stretcher each morning and rolled him all over the hospital.

His favorite place to visit was a window overlooking a construction site. Scottish Rite was in the midst of a huge building project that would practically double the size of the hospital. Like giant ladles, enormous yellow earthmovers scooped up the Georgia red clay and deposited it in the belly of a dump truck. Bulldozers crawled back and forth all day pushing and shoving the dirt. Jonathan was mesmerized. Even though he had to remain flat on his back, he begged me to position him in front of the window each morning where he waved vigorously at the busy workers. They energetically waved back at him, flattered by the loyal attention from their one and only fan. After days of observing the construction activity, he made a monumental decision: he would be a construction worker when he grew up.

April 1 rolled around and provided a happy diversion for Jonathan. His playful, mischievous personality erupted full-force, teasing everyone and entertaining them with "April Fool" jokes. For weeks, he had harassed his doctors endlessly about when he could finally eat pizza. On April 1 when his surgeon made his hospital rounds, Jonathan eagerly awaited his visit. "Guess what? Last night mom brought me some pizza for dinner and it was really yummy!" He was struggling not to burst out laughing. The doctor jerked his head up from Jonathan's medical chart with a look of horror written all over his face. I was afraid he might kill both of us before Jonathan hollered out, "April Fool!" Jonathan had been on clear liquids and IV feedings for so long it was a miracle that his sense of humor was still intact!

On April 2, just four days from surgery, Jonathan began vomiting and running a fever. By April 4 he could not even keep down Tylenol, and his fever was up to 104 degrees. Prior to surgery, he would need to take several doses of an oral antibiotic. We knew if he were too sick to take the antibiotic, we would need to postpone his surgery—again. The doctor prescribed suppositories to help combat the nausea and the fever. I felt completely exhausted and emotionally defeated.

The old adage, "if it can go wrong, it will," was certainly proving true. Every time his surgery date drew near, new setbacks cropped up. I pleaded with God for answers and understanding. Once again, we called our church and Sunday school friends and rallied the troops to pray for Jonathan. By 4:00 p.m. the day before surgery, Jonathan had managed to keep one dose of the antibiotic down. We had two more doses to go before surgery.

My parents were flying in to be with us for the surgery, and they arrived that evening along with Dan, a church staff member, and his wife. Dan could tell with one look that we were all emotionally hanging by a thread. He suggested we completely encircle Jonathan's bed, join hands, and pray. One by one, we offered up prayers for Jonathan's healing and expressions of thanksgiving for God's constant abiding grace. The memory of that day will forever linger in my mind. We sensed God's presence in that room in a powerful way. The tension from weeks of worry slowly drained away and a calm assurance that the Great Physician would take control took its place.

From that moment on, Jonathan's nausea disappeared and the fever dissipated. He managed to keep down the last two doses of the antibiotic as well as some liquids. Surgery remained on schedule for the next day.

The following morning I heard the orderlies rolling the stretcher towards our room long before the sun peeked through the window. Jonathan had been sick for the previous eight months and hospitalized for most of that time, but barring any further delays, he would soon be on the road to recovery. So many conflicting emotions darted through my head. Johnny and I followed the stretcher down the long hallway to the OR entrance with one of us on either side grasping Jonathan's hands. "We'll be waiting for you as soon as you wake up," we assured him. We barely had time for one last kiss before the orderlies rushed him through the mysterious OR doors.

Johnny and I quickly gulped breakfast in the hospital dining room then made our way upstairs to the hospital chapel for a time of prayer. We then gathered in Jonathan's room along with my parents and friends who had begun to arrive and prepared for a long wait.

That day I experienced first-hand how helpful it is to have people to talk to while waiting for surgery to be over. There was not a minute from early in the morning until Jonathan's surgery ended that we were alone. Most of the day, the room was full to overflowing with nurses dragging in every unoccupied chair on the floor for our visitors. They came and went all day long, lavishing us with food, books, magazines, toys for Jonathan, and most importantly, their love and prayers and the gift of their presence.

Marsha spent her lunch hour in the operating room and came back to report that everything was going fine. Someone from OR also called us every hour reassuring us that all was well.

Finally, around 4:00 p.m. after eight hours of surgery, Jonathan's surgeon called to report that it was over. They had removed his entire colon, created the ileostomy, and repositioned his central-line catheter. They had not been able to remove the lining from the twelve-inch area that remained because there was too much inflammation. However, he assured us that he could take care of that sometime in the future. Everyone in the OR had been amazed at the extent of the disease that had destroyed his colon. The inflammation throughout his entire colon had been so severe that the fever he had experienced prior to surgery had most likely stemmed from that area.

Relief washed over my entire being like a spring in the desert. All the days and months spent in the hospital and all the setbacks we had encountered no longer mattered. All that mattered now was his recovery. After he had healed sufficiently, probably six months to a year, he would have one more operation to remove the lining from the twelve remaining inches of his colon and to close off his ileostomy bag. Then we would be home free. We could finally see the light at the end of the tunnel. We couldn't wait to see him and tell him the good news.

Jonathan's surgeon had attempted to explain to us in advance what to expect following surgery, but nothing could have prepared me for his totally altered appearance. Jonathan's face was swollen and pale; he had a tube down his nose to pump fluids from his stomach, another tube coming from his bladder, a heart and respirator monitor, IV's everywhere, bags of fluids and medicines hanging from multiple IV monitors, and both of his hands tied down to prevent him from pulling out the tubes and IV's while he was still under the influence of the anesthesia. I hardly recognized him. We sat with him until the nurses shooed us out, and even though he slept, he occasionally squeezed my fingers assuring me that he was okay.

Jonathan stayed in ICU overnight, returning to his room the next morning. The nurses had taped a huge poster to the wall above his bed that read: "WELCOME BACK JONATHAN. WE LOVE YOU!" They had drawn comical caricatures of themselves at the bottom of the poster.

Over the following days, the doctor removed most of his tubes. Though he wasn't ready for pizza yet, he was definitely inching closer.

Chapter 6

A Peaceful Summer

Jonathan's rapid recovery surprised everyone. His stress fracture still prevented him from being able to walk, but overall he improved daily. His doctors gradually reduced his medications, and he tolerated soft foods well. His doctor left his incision open to heal from the inside out because of his weight gain prior to surgery and because of the risk of infection. It was a raw, angry-looking, deep, vertical wound, approximately nine inches long, stuffed with patches of gauze. A horrible sight! I had never seen anything like it. The first time I observed the nurse changing the dressing, I began to feel light-headed and feared that I would pass out. He looked like he had been in a sword fight and had lost the battle. Jonathan, however, was actually quite proud of his wound.

The month of May brought a bit of notoriety for Jonathan. Someone from the Atlanta-Journal-Constitution newspaper approached Scottish Rite Hospital about writing an article dealing with a critically ill child who had spent a lot of time in the hospital. Guess who perfectly fit that description. A reporter and cameraman arrived at Jonathan's room early one morning. They interviewed each of us and took pictures. Jonathan strutted like a celebrity. A few days later our family appeared on the front page of the "Lifestyle" section of the Atlanta Journal-Constitution.

Several interesting events occurred as a result of that article. Much to his delight, Jonathan began to receive a lot of mail and phone calls from total strangers. One day a letter arrived from an elderly woman named Hattie Mae who said she was praying for Jonathan and wanted to send him some money to buy something he would enjoy. Enclosed was a ten-dollar bill. It was the first of many encouraging letters from Hattie Mae. She was a real prayer warrior, and we looked forward to her letters, though we were never able to meet her in person. We also received a phone call from friends at our previous church that we hadn't seen in over twelve years.

The cloud of despondency that had hung over our heads for months finally began to lift. On May 15, 1982, Jonathan was finally able to leave the hospital. He had been a patient since February 16, almost three months to the day without going home. That definitely called for a celebration. The nurses surprised him with a "going home" party complete with cake and ice cream that he could finally eat. The doctors, therapists, custodial staff—even Sonny, one of the hospital pharmacists—came to tell Jonathan goodbye and to remind him to return only to visit until time for his final surgery. They had cared for and loved our entire family. We would miss them.

We arrived home to another celebration. Our neighbors had once again hung a huge "WELCOME HOME" sign at our garage door, framed on each side by clusters of rainbow-colored balloons. They had gathered in our driveway to welcome Jonathan home. It was a cause for celebration.

Summer approached rapidly, and Jonathan was on the mend. My heart overflowed with gratitude to God for answered prayers. Jonathan was beginning to walk again by the end of June, though he still lacked stamina. He also adjusted amazingly well to his ileostomy bag, even learning how to change and empty it himself.

I was somewhat apprehensive about his beginning first grade in August with the ostomy bag, but I refused to let my fears dampen my spirits. The glorious promise of summer lay before us, and we could not have been happier. I looked forward to spending time with Jamie and Jonathan. I worried that Jamie had gotten lost in the shuffle over the previous year while we were so preoccupied with Jonathan. She never complained and was as eager for Jonathan to be well as we were, but I knew she deserved some of my undivided attention. She was growing up so fast. We wanted that summer to be a happy one for her as well as for Jonathan. She had planned to spend part of her summer at church camp and on choir tour, and I desperately wanted the two of us to spend some quality time together doing "girl stuff."

By mid-summer, Jonathan could tolerate a normal diet, even hamburgers and pizza. His doctor had slowly weaned him off the cortisone medication, and he had lost the extra weight. Thankfully, his stamina had gradually improved. We decided a vacation would do us all a world of good.

A friend suggested that Williamsburg, Virginia would be a great place to relax and tour at our own pace. We had been using a wheelchair for Jonathan since he could not walk long distances. Williamsburg's paved walkways seemed ideal for our situation. We loaded our luggage in the car and headed out for a week of relaxation.

One particular afternoon, we had been touring for several hours and Jonathan had been in his wheelchair for quite some time. Right in the middle of a very crowded area, he decided to get up out of his chair and walk. As people began to stare at him walking away from his wheelchair, Jamie didn't miss a beat. In her best evangelistic voice she yelled, "Thank you, Lord. He's been healed! It's a miracle!" She always loved drama.

Jamie and Jonathan devoted the remainder of that summer to relaxing at home and playing with the neighborhood kids. One morning I looked out the front window just in time to see Jonathan rolling sideways down the hill in front of our house. Over and over he rolled with his friends trailing right behind him. What was he thinking! His ostomy bag could have sprung a leak or worse yet completely fallen off. I raced to the door fully intending to scold him. Suddenly I stopped abruptly in my tracks. I had to quit constantly hovering over him and allow him to be normal. I had worried about his health for so long it was almost impossible to let go and give him the freedom just to be a normal six-year-old boy.

Chapter 7

Charlie

The refreshing days of summer sped by quickly. Jonathan would soon enter first grade so I decided to schedule a meeting with his elementary school principal. I called, and we agreed to meet a couple of weeks prior to school starting.

Even though I thought it might be helpful for the principal to meet Jonathan, I didn't want Jonathan listening to our discussion of how ill he had been during the prior year. I decided to leave him at home with Jamie and attend the meeting alone.

The principal welcomed me into his office, and his infectious smile immediately put me at ease. He was a kindly man in his late forties who obviously loved his vocation. He remembered when Jamie had attended his school and he reminisced for a while about what a good student she had been, how she had made excellent grades and had never been a behavior problem, and how much he looked forward to having her brother for a student. I mentally congratulated myself for deciding to leave Jonathan at home. The principal would learn soon enough that Jamie and Jonathan were as different as night and day.

Knowing how busy he had to be just days before school began, I got right to the point. I explained in as much detail as I thought he could handle how very sick Jonathan had been and the emotional toll it had taken on our entire family. I carefully laid out all of my concerns about Jonathan starting first grade with an ileostomy bag. I explained that he might need to go to the bathroom at unscheduled times to empty it. "My purpose in meeting with you today is certainly not to ask to select his teacher myself," I explained, "but I am asking that you give careful consideration to placing him with a patient, understanding, and loving teacher." He leaned back in his chair and gave me a broad smile.

"You have nothing to worry about, Mrs. Flanders," he exclaimed. "All of our teachers are patient, understanding, and loving. You know, a close relative of mine who is in her fifties has a colostomy. She has done remarkably well, and I'm sure Jonathan will do fine also." He was totally missing the point. *I'll bet it's been awhile since you saw her rolling sideways down a long hill with her colostomy bag attached,* I thought to myself. However, remembering that I was after all a Christian and needed to behave accordingly, I gave him my best smile and pretended to be reassured by our little meeting.

School began on August 25, which also happened to be my birthday, but I was too nervous about Jonathan beginning school to think about celebrating. I drove him to school the first day and met his teacher, Mrs. Murphy. My meeting with the principal had not been in vain after all. Mrs. Murphy was wonderful. She truly was patient, understanding, and loving. She promised to call me if there were any problems with Jonathan's bag. When he was out of the room, she discussed his unique situation with the rest of the children in his class to help them understand and to prevent any teasing or ridicule. She treated him like any other student in the class. One of his best friends from church, Kenny Hutson, was also in his class, which provided an added bonus.

I should have learned by that time never to underestimate Jonathan's ability to survive any situation. At the end of his first week of school, I asked him if everything had gone well and if he'd had any problems with his ostomy bag that he needed to talk to me about. "Oh, you mean Charlie?" he asked.

"Charlie! Who is Charlie?" I didn't remember anyone in his class named Charlie.

"Charlie is my ostomy bag," he explained. "All the kids want to see it."

"They do!" I was struggling not to look as horrified as I felt. "What do you tell them?"

"I tell them they can see Charlie if they give me some money, and I've made a lot of money this week." He was grinning from ear to ear, and obviously quite pleased with his entrepreneurial skills. I was speechless. And to think I had spent all summer fretting and worrying about his adjustment. I had to spend a considerable amount of time on my knees apologizing to God for my lack of faith.

Jonathan loved school and actually did very well. Our first parent-teacher conference revealed that the only problem he had experienced had had nothing to do with his health, but had resulted from a personality trait he unfortunately inherited from me—he enjoyed talking much more than he liked listening. Mrs. Murphy politely commented that he was extremely "social." I broke out in laughter. I knew that was "teacher-talk" for "he talks non-stop all day long." His social skills were, unfortunately, interfering with his schoolwork. He failed to complete almost every assignment. I promised his teacher we would find a solution.

Jonathan had always performed best when offered a reward for achievement as opposed to punishment for poor performance. It didn't take long to find an excellent motivator. The original *Star Wars* movie had made its debut in 1977, and Jonathan had become the movie's number one fan. He had an obsession with everything connected with *Star Wars*. He loved R2D2, C3PO, Chewbacca, and of course, Princess Lea. He played his *Star Wars* cassette tape over and over until he had memorized the entire tape. Actually, everyone in our family had memorized it because we had heard it so often. On mornings when he refused to get out of bed, Jamie played the *Star Wars* theme song on the piano, and he hopped right up. We decided to reward him with a new *Star Wars* figure at the end of each week if he had completed every assignment for that week. Yes, I know it reeked of bribery, but it couldn't have worked better. He began bringing home "smiley" faces almost immediately, and his *Star Wars* collection grew rapidly.

Chapter 8

Disease Strikes Again

Our idyllic days of good health for Jonathan were short-lived. The hemorrhaging returned with a vengeance only a few short weeks after weaning him off all medication. The swiftness and aggressiveness of the ulcerative colitis that recurred in the remaining twelve inches of his colon was appalling.

Jonathan's gastroenterologist began treating him with a new medication that had proven to show promise with ulcerative colitis. However, not only did Jonathan fail to improve, his condition actually worsened. The doctor promptly discontinued the new medication and resumed his cortisone medications. Jonathan was on adult dosages of prednisone, which caused his weight to balloon overnight. He literally had three chins and could barely walk because of the added weight. One of the side effects of the cortisone medication he had taken for so long was facial swelling and puffiness. The cortisone medication altered his facial features, giving him a strange, abnormal appearance. I dreaded taking him out in public. Everywhere we went people gawked and stared and made cruel comments about his weight and appearance.

One evening when Johnny came home from work, he found Jonathan sitting quietly near the fireplace. One look at his expression told Johnny something was terribly wrong. He dropped to one knee placing his arms around Jonathan. "Buddy, did anything happen at school today that upset you?" Jonathan burst into tears. He was crying so hard it was difficult to understand what he was saying.

"When I got on the bus to go to school today a boy called me 'frog face.' Do I look funny, Daddy?" Johnny pulled him down into his lap cradling him, rubbing his back, and sobbing with him. Johnny's heart was broken. The overwhelming sadness of the moment carved a permanent memory in Johnny's heart. From that day forward, we drove Jonathan to and from school and avoided the school bus. By November, his condition had deteriorated to the point that it became necessary for him to drop out of school entirely and rely on a homebound teacher.

My heart grieved for him, and I became almost paralyzed with fear. His condition grew worse each day. The constant hemorrhaging left his sheets covered with blood almost every morning.

One night as Johnny and I lay in bed unable to sleep, I began to sob uncontrollably. The burden of watching my perfectly normal little boy physically deteriorate right before my eyes was more than I could bear. Cancer, the disease that I had feared the most, could not have been any worse than that. I was his mother, and I should have been able to do something to help him. Yet I could not. A fear that had been embedded deep in my sub-conscious for many months suddenly rose to the surface. The words that I had feared to verbalize tumbled out. "What if he doesn't make it this time? What if we enter his room one morning only to discover he is no longer with us? Why hasn't God healed him?" There were no answers, and God was strangely silent.

I wrote in my prayer journal November 3, 1982:

Lord, if you are trying to teach us something, please help us to listen to Your voice and be willing to learn from You. I completely relinquish Jonathan to You this very day. I understand that You may miraculously heal him or You may choose not to. Only You know the scope of Jonathan's life and Your ultimate purpose for him. I place him completely in Your hands and totally submit to Your will.

That prayer of relinquishment was not always easy to pray, but I began to pray it daily. And we did start to see some improvement. Jonathan's surgeon felt it was time to remove the lining from the twelve remaining inches of his colon, because his disease had returned so aggressively. Since the disease had attacked the lining, removing it would prevent him from ever having ulcerative colitis again. There was just one catch; he had to be free of the disease in that area before his doctor could remove the lining. The surgeon had also planned to create an internal pouch that would serve as a reservoir for his intestinal output. This was a new surgical procedure never before performed at Scottish Rite. If successful, it would allow him to close off Jonathan's ostomy bag permanently. We could say goodbye to "Charlie" forever. We scheduled his surgery for December 15, fully aware that he would probably spend the Christmas season in the hospital. It seemed a small price to pay to see him finally well.

Jonathan entered the hospital on December 14. He had improved, but tests revealed that he was not yet well enough for surgery. After a week in the hospital enduring the all too familiar treatments, Jonathan's doctors decided once again to delay the surgery and allow him to go home for Christmas. His doctor rescheduled his surgery for the first week in January, allowing him another two weeks to heal and permitting him to celebrate Christmas at home. His condition required even more medication. His happy, playful personality seemed hidden under the mask of the medications and the disease. My little trooper who had always been singing and laughing seemed enveloped in sadness and silence.

We didn't leave the house very often because rest was critical to his recovery, but his best friend, Kenny, invited him to his birthday party in December, and Jonathan begged to go. Hoping it would lift his spirits to see his friends, I drove him the short distance to Kenny's house. It broke my heart that he was so weak he could only sit and watch while his friends played.

We weren't sure what to do about Christmas. We had planned to make our annual trip to my parents' home in Mississippi, but Jonathan was too weak to make the long journey by car. Jonathan's surgeon agreed that he could go if we could fly there. However, there was simply no way we could stretch our budget to allow all of us to travel by plane. We had struggled to make ends meet during the prior year with the loss of my income and the medical bills piling up daily. We finally decided Jonathan and I would fly, and Johnny and Jamie would go by car.

That was Jonathan's first plane ride, and we expected excitement and anticipation. Before he had become sick, he had been fascinated with the idea of flying in an airplane. Nothing would have thrilled him more. His lack of excitement, however, revealed how very sick he was. I determined that when his health returned, we would fly anywhere he wanted to go so he could enjoy it to the fullest.

We boarded the plane a few days before Christmas for the short flight. The well-trained flight attendant realized Jonathan was not well and showered him with extra attention. She pinned a small plastic airplane on his shirt and fussed over him with sodas and bags of peanuts. He was again on a very restricted diet, so I promised to save his peanuts for a special treat after his surgery. The flight ended quickly. My parents met us at the airport, and I could tell from the look on their faces that they were alarmed about Jonathan's appearance and medical condition.

I felt very little joy in my heart as we celebrated the birth of Christ. All I could focus on was getting through the holidays as fast as possible so we could get his surgery behind us. Jonathan had shown little interest that year in creating a list for Santa, but we knew when he was well his *Star Wars* obsession would rekindle. He rewarded us with the biggest smile we had seen in weeks when he saw the *Star Wars* figures and space ships he had received for Christmas. The new Atari game that was the latest rage also managed to create more excitement with Jamie and Jonathan than we had seen in a while.

We had an appointment with Jonathan's surgeon shortly after we returned home. Jonathan's condition had not improved, and we expected his doctor to postpone his surgery yet again. We knew that he was critically ill, but we were not prepared to hear the doctor's assessment. Jonathan's medical condition had deteriorated to the point that he could not live much longer without the surgery, but there was no guarantee he would survive the surgery. I understood why his doctor had permitted him to be with his grandparents and other relatives during the Christmas holidays; he had feared it might be his last Christmas. I cried softly as Johnny urged the doctor to do everything possible to save him. We entered the hospital the following day to prepare him for surgery. The surgery was scheduled for January 5, 1983, just six days before his seventh birthday. We knew the doctor would not postpone the surgery again.

Chapter 9

Sixteen-Hour Surgery

Jonathan had a good day the day before surgery. He worked puzzles and played with his *Star Wars* toys. Thankfully, we occupied our minds with friends dropping by to visit. I spent the night at Scottish Rite with him, and he stayed awake playing late into the evening.

I lay awake long after Jonathan went to sleep. My mind refused to accept the fact that he might not survive the surgery. I focused instead on thanking God for allowing us to be Jonathan and Jamie's parents, for providing everything we had needed, and for all the miracles we had already witnessed. I picked up my Bible, and with only the soft glow from the room night-light, I sought comfort in the Psalms. Deep into the night, I continued to gather strength and comfort from God's Word. Finally, I prayed the prayer I had prayed daily, relinquishing Jonathan totally into God's care. Eventually sleep came.

Marsha was the nurse assigned to him that day, and she came early to bathe and prep him for surgery. He was in a good mood and seemed to have blotted from his mind the fact that surgery loomed imminent.

Marsha administered an injection around 9:00 a.m., causing reality to set in. He began to cry and say he didn't want to go to surgery. Fear squeezed out any semblance of calm. I held him close and gently rocked him in my arms. I had no way of knowing if that would be my last time to hold him and tell him how much I loved him or how proud I was to be his mother. I began to softly sing his favorite nursery rhymes and gently rub his back. He quickly drifted off to sleep in my arms.

He barely roused when the orderlies arrived thirty minutes later and lifted him onto the gurney. Just as before when he had been to surgery, we followed along holding his hands as far as the orderlies allowed us to go, then kissed him good-bye. Friends had already begun to gather when we returned to his room.

Someone called us from the operating room every hour with an update, but the day progressed very slowly. The OR nurse assured us that he was fine, but the surgery was taking longer than expected—much longer. At 5:00 p.m. a call came from the OR informing us that they were still a long way from being through. They had encountered much more inflammation than they had anticipated. Removing the lining from the twelve-inch area of his colon was very slow and tedious because of the inflammation; if even a microscopic piece remained, the disease could return.

A friend brought Jamie to the hospital after school and also brought dinner to us, though eating was the farthest thing from our minds. According to his doctors, his surgery should have lasted about four hours. Jonathan had been in surgery over nine hours, and we desperately needed to see him and know that he was okay.

By 11:00 p.m. everyone who had come to the hospital to wait with us had gone home. We were becoming frantic about the length of the surgery. I had never heard of anyone being in surgery that long. My mind lingered on the possible consequences of being under anesthesia that many hours. Surely, no one could survive that, especially someone as weak as Jonathan had been going into surgery. Johnny and I paced back and forth. At midnight, we decided to walk over to the OR area and wait outside the door they would be wheeling him through when the surgery was over. I had an overwhelming desire to storm through the OR doors and see for myself that he was okay.

Finally, at 2:00 a.m., the heavy OR doors sprang open, and they wheeled Jonathan out of surgery and into ICU. We were weeping from relief. He had miraculously survived 16 ½ hours of surgery.

He actually looked better than we had expected after being on the operating table that many hours, or maybe we knew better what to expect because of his previous surgery. Completely overcome with exhaustion, his surgeon could barely stand up straight. Even though several surgeons and surgical residents had rotated shifts, he had not left the operating room except for meals and short breaks. I'm sure he wanted nothing more than to go home and sleep for hours, but he sat down with us and explained why the surgery had taken so long and patiently answered all of our questions. He assured us that Jonathan's vital signs had remained stable throughout the entire operation. He had successfully removed all of the lining from his colon; however, because that part of the surgery had taken so long, he had not been able to close off his ostomy bag. That would require further surgery, but it should be minor compared to what he had already endured. Then he gave us the news we had waited a year-and-a-half to hear: Jonathan no longer had ulcerative colitis. His operation provided a surgical cure for that debilitating disease, and he would never have ulcerative colitis again. It had been a long time coming, but it was music to our ears. Our spirits danced though our bodies were too exhausted to move. We hugged his doctor and thanked him, then sent him home for some much-needed rest.

All that remained now was for Jonathan to completely recover and undergo the final surgery to close off his ileostomy bag. All the stress and tension of the past year-and-a-half would be behind us and pushed to the farthest corners of our minds. We could finally get on with our lives.

Before Johnny took Jamie home, we joined hands and thanked God that the surgery had been successful and that his disease had finally been defeated. We had no clue in those early morning hours that more dark storms were headed our way—darker than anything we had experienced so far. Our joy was to be very short-lived.

Chapter 10

I'll See You in the Morning

Part of the construction at Scottish Rite included building a new ICU. At the time of Jonathan's surgery, a temporary ICU occupied the top floor of the hospital. Previously used as regular patient rooms, the entire floor was vacant except for ICU patients. All of the ICU patients except Jonathan were premature babies housed in one large room on the top floor. In order for us to stay with Jonathan all day, his doctor placed him in a regular patient room a short distance from the large room that housed the other ICU patients. Nurses rotated shifts in his room providing constant care twenty-four hours a day. We had permission to stay with him all day, but because of the vast array of medical equipment in his room, we could not stay with him overnight. His surgeon arranged for us to sleep in a vacant room next to Jonathan's room.

The morning following his surgery, after Johnny and Jamie had gone home, I attempted to catch up on some much-needed sleep. I slept restlessly in spite of being exhausted from the previous day. After tossing and turning for several hours, I got up and entered Jonathan's room around 6:00 a.m. He was doing fairly well, but the nurses were closely monitoring his pulse rate and blood pressure. Both were starting to rise. His pulse had risen to 180 and his blood pressure was 150/115. He slept most of the day, but occasionally opened his eyes and squeezed my hand.

Friday, January 7, two days following his surgery, Johnny spent the night at the hospital. Jonathan was still drowsy from the surgery and anesthesia and slept most of the night. His vital signs remained elevated, and his nurses monitored his condition closely. Jamie and I ran some errands Saturday morning and caught up on some things at home, then arrived at the hospital around 3:00 p.m. Apparently, the anesthesia had finally worn off. We were relieved to see Jonathan alert and almost his "old self." He was completely focused on his upcoming seventh birthday on January 11, and since he had lost track of time, he quizzed us relentlessly. "How many days till my birthday? Can I have a party? Can my friends come? Will I get new *Star Wars* toys? Will the doctors let me eat birthday cake?"

His excitement was contagious. We decided to let him open one present early—a *Star Wars* Trash Compactor—to celebrate his surgery being over. His excitement over his new *Star Wars* toy helped to ease my tension from the previous days. I finally gave my body permission to relax.

It was my turn to spend the night on Saturday. I stayed in Jonathan's room talking and laughing with him until I realized it was past 11:00 p.m. It was wonderful to see him happy and alert; we were both reluctant to call it a night. At 11:30 he was still talking and watching television. I knew he needed his rest, so I assured him if he would turn off the TV and go to sleep, I would be right next door. If he awoke and needed me, the nurse would come and get me. He said, "No, Mommy. Let's just watch TV and talk a little while longer. Please don't leave." I could not refuse those big brown eyes.

"Just a few more minutes, okay?" Finally, around midnight he drifted off to sleep. He briefly opened his eyes as I softly kissed him goodnight and rubbed his face. "I love you so much, Jonathan, and I'm so thankful you're getting well. I'll see you in the morning."

"I'll see you in the morning, Mommy," he murmured as he drifted back to sleep.

As long as I live on this earth, I'll forever regret that I left his room that night. I had no way of knowing that that would be the last meaningful conversation I would ever have with my son.

His nurse informed me that Jonathan was her only patient that night, so he would have her undivided attention. She promised to awaken me if he needed me.

I awoke early Sunday morning, January 9, showered and dressed quickly and entered Jonathan's room around 7:30. His evening nurse had already ended her shift, and his morning nurse only worked weekends so I had never met her before. I walked around to Jonathan's bed and gave him a kiss. "Good morning, Jonathan. Did you sleep well?" His eyes were open and appeared normal, but he did not respond. "Jonathan, how are you feeling this morning?" I asked a little louder. Still no response.

"Did he speak to you?" his nurse asked.

"No, his eyes are open but he seems to be staring vacantly into space," I replied.

"I don't think he's responding normally this morning," she said. "I've called his doctor."

Suddenly, his chin began to quiver, his eyes rolled back, and he began to shake violently all over. His body shook so hard his entire bed vibrated, and the multiple glass IV bottles clanged together loudly, threatening to crash into each other. Something had gone terribly wrong. Fear gripped my heart and wrapped its tentacles around my soul, threatening to squeeze the very life from me. Jonathan's surgeon rushed into his room and took immediate action. He began vociferously yelling out orders to the nurse in rapid-fire succession while at the same time administering phenobarbital and valium. The shaking stopped almost instantly, and Jonathan went limp.

I stood by completely helpless and in a state of shock. Jonathan's doctor pulled me aside. "Jonathan has just experienced a grand mal seizure. His vital signs are deteriorating rapidly. We need to intubate him and get him on a ventilator immediately. I've called in some additional specialists to help stabilize him, but I'm going to have to ask you to wait outside his room. You need to call Johnny—and you might want to call the prayer team from your church."

I reluctantly left Jonathan's room as the doctor closed the door and left me trembling alone in the hall. Before I could even pull myself together enough to find the nearest phone, doctors began pouring into my little boy's room. His gastro doctor entered his room wearing a grim expression. He had enlisted the help of a kidney specialist because Jonathan's body fluids were fluctuating wildly and were totally out of balance. A neurologist arrived shortly thereafter. As doctors and nurses rushed in, I could see through the door that the surgeon was holding Jonathan's chin and pumping oxygen into his body— "bagging" him—until they could connect him to the ventilator. It seemed impossible just hours earlier he had been laughing, joking, and teasing me about staying up so late. He now appeared lifeless and near death.

I managed to find a phone and called Johnny. He took the time to make one call to our church then rushed to the hospital. I desperately needed the comfort of his arms around me reassuring me that God loved Jonathan even more than we did and promising me that everything would be all right.

Johnny's faith has always been like the Rock of Gibraltar. I've always been able to draw from his strength, even when my own faith has ebbed. Johnny is the calmest, most even-tempered person I've ever known. He rarely gets angry, and I've never heard him say an unkind word about anyone. I had admired and respected his unwavering faith in the Lord before we had ever dated.

During the long months of Jonathan's illness, hospital chaplains and chaplains-in-training had flowed in and out of our room at Scottish Rite. One chaplain had shared with us that when a child is critically ill; the emotional strain that the illness places on the family frequently causes the family to seek divorce. We had witnessed the truth of that in many of the families that we had met while Jonathan had been a patient.

Our situation had actually had the reverse effect. Our overwhelming sense of desperation and inadequacy had drawn us closer to one another as we daily stormed heaven's gates together pleading with God on Jonathan's behalf.

I needed to be able to draw from Johnny's strength that day more than ever before. All morning the doctors and nurses had come and gone from Jonathan's room. Portable x-ray equipment, monitors, and all kinds of hospital machinery rolled in and out of his room. A large crowd of friends had gathered by then to wait with us and support us.

Finally, one of the doctors emerged from Jonathan's room to talk with us. "Jonathan is sedated and now on the ventilator. The two of you may go in and see him for a few minutes. We cannot give you a prognosis at this point, but we are attempting to stabilize him. We're doing everything we can for him at this moment."

We opened the door, went in, and slammed emotionally head-on into a disconcerting reality. Jonathan laid still and silent, totally unaware that we were even in the room. No one told us initially, no one had to, that following the seizure, he had slipped into a coma. I felt numb all over. *Surely, this must be a bad dream, and I will awaken soon to see Jonathan laughing and playing.* Unfortunately, it was all too real.

The neurologist came out to talk with us that afternoon. "We are just not sure what triggered the seizure. We gradually weaned him off the cortisone medication, his blood pressure and pulse were abnormally high, and his fluids were out of balance. Any of those conditions or the combination could have triggered it. We may never know for sure. As soon as he is stable, we will take him for a CAT scan just to make sure he hasn't sustained any permanent brain damage. In the meantime, we will keep him on a low dosage of phenobarbitol to prevent any additional seizures." He said it all so calmly—so matter of fact—as though the very life of my child were not at stake. My mind heard everything he had said, but my heart refused to accept it. We served an all-powerful God—the Great Physician—and He would heal our son completely. I was sure of it.

Jonathan's surgeon stayed with him all day. He left briefly in the evening to go home for dinner, returning later with an overnight bag. He informed the ICU nurse that he would be spending the night down the hall close to Jonathan's room. He instructed her to summon him immediately any time during the night if Jonathan took a turn for the worse.

If there had been any doubt in our minds as to the seriousness of Jonathan's condition, that confirmed it. The doctor also arranged for his partner to take all of his cases until Jonathan's condition stabilized. He planned to devote all of his time to our son. We had never heard of a doctor with this level of commitment to his patient. We knew he would do everything in his power to restore Jonathan to health.

Johnny and I both spent that night at the hospital. We arranged for Jamie to stay with a friend. We stayed awake in Jonathan's room all night, praying for a miracle.

Chapter 11

Whack a Mole

As his seventh birthday rolled around on January 11, 1983, Jonathan remained comatose, his heart rate and blood pressure continued to stay elevated, and his body fluids fluctuated dangerously. And if that wasn't enough, a heart specialist detected irregular heartbeats and ordered a series of EKGs. We discovered that Jonathan had begun to experience PVCs—skipped heartbeats that could potentially be very serious.

His team of specialists convened to discuss his multiple problems. The cardiologist suggested that perhaps his central-line catheter (his internal catheter used to administrate medications and IV feedings and to draw blood cultures) could possibly be causing his irregular heartbeats. Sure enough, an x-ray revealed that his central-line had looped over inside a heart valve causing his irregular heartbeats. Jonathan's surgeon brought the necessary equipment to Jonathan's room the next morning and pulled the line back an inch or so. That seemed to solve the problem. However, another equally serious problem presented itself overnight. His blood count and platelets had begun to drop. His doctor, obviously worried, ordered an immediate blood transfusion. He had to find the cause of this new development quickly.

A hematologist rounded out the growing list of doctors attending to Jonathan's needs. After studying Jonathan's lab values, she asked us to join her in the conference room to discuss this new development. "There are numerous situations that could cause a drop in blood platelets," she explained. "It could be something as simple as a reaction to one of the five antibiotics he has been taking since before the surgery to prevent infection or something as serious as hemorrhaging in the brain or somewhere else internally. We'll begin by eliminating the antibiotics to see if that corrects the situation." Thankfully, the antibiotics proved to be the culprit. Discontinuing the antibiotics brought his blood count and platelets back in the normal range.

We were thankful that those two problems were resolved, but we were daily fighting fires, medically speaking. As soon as we solved one problem, another cropped up. It reminded me of an arcade game called "Whack a Mole" that Jonathan and Jamie had enjoyed playing. The object of the game was to use a huge rubber hammer to whack a pretend mole that was sticking its head up through a hole in the game table. The catch was that every time the player whacked the mole with the hammer, another mole popped up, then another, and another, etc. There seemed to be no end in sight to Jonathan's medical problems.

It seemed inconceivable that just three days before, Jonathan had been happily planning his birthday party. As I dressed to go to the hospital the morning of the eleventh, my eyes fell on the stack of colorfully wrapped birthday presents that we had purchased before his surgery in anticipation of a joyful celebration. There was no point in taking them to him. The festive wrapping paper and bright bows only reminded me that there was no joy, no celebration. I hastily stuffed the gifts into his closet, not wanting any reminders of the sadness surrounding his seventh birthday.

That day I hit rock bottom. Alone with Jonathan in his ICU room, I tried to form the words to pray for him, but my throat choked up and my eyes filled with tears. Sorrow gripped my heart like a vise; the words would not come. I lay across his bed and wept. I missed him desperately and longed to hear his happy chatter. I heard footsteps in the hall and looked up to see his nurse enter the room.

"I need to speak with you out in the hall," she commanded.

Thinking there was some new development, I dried my eyes, blew my nose and followed her out the door.

"It is important that you not cry in front of Jonathan," she blurted out. "We don't know what he hears and comprehends, so it is important that you be positive and cheerful in his presence at all times."

With that "dressing down," she turned on her heels and left. I was furious! I knew what she said was right, but I had an overwhelming desire to shout, "When do I get to cry? When is it my turn to grieve? I'm with him all day, and I don't feel cheerful and positive. I feel sad, and brokenhearted, and terrified."

I knew she meant well, but I desperately needed someone to gather me in a hug and tell me everything would be okay.

Surely, the worst was behind us, and we would begin to see improvement any day now. Unfortunately, nothing could have been further from the truth. The storm that had blown into our lives had just begun to unleash its fury. We would need to cling tightly to our faith to survive the days ahead.

At the suggestion of our neurologist, we began to talk to Jonathan and sing his favorite songs. We brought his *Star Wars* cassette tape and played it over and over to try to stimulate him mentally. We even physically propped him up in bed with one of us behind him supporting his back and pretended to play Atari by holding his fingers and manipulating the knobs for him. He and Jamie had spent hours playing "Frogger" when he was well. He had squealed with delight every time he managed to get the frog across the street with no mishaps. Jamie now sat patiently and tried to play with him, but there was no reaction whatsoever. Zero. His body, still swollen from the cortisone medications, continued to show no response, and he had a dull, blank, lifeless expression that never changed. His eyes that had once been so alive appeared to register nothing. He was somewhere very far away. It broke my heart to see how hard Jamie tried to help him, and how gently she treated him even though he showed no response.

He did not even react to pain. Occasionally, the phlebotomist attempted to get blood specimens by inserting a needle into his arm instead of using his central-line catheter. There was no response whatsoever.

About four days after his seizure, I noticed that his left leg was slightly swollen and turning blue. I brought it to the nurse's attention.

"It may be a little swollen, but it's hard to tell. We'll watch it," she responded.

I knew the symptoms of a blood clot, having been down that road before, and I insisted that she call Jonathan's doctor. It did indeed prove to be a blood clot. For the first time, we saw the doctor let his guard down. He took us into an empty room and sat down on the bed.

"You need to know that if the clot travels it could be fatal." Then he did something totally out of character. He put his head in his hands and told us how sorry he was for everything that had happened to Jonathan.

"I've been over and over his entire past year-and-a-half in my mind, and I don't know of anything we could have done differently. I've done everything I know to do medically for Jonathan. You and Johnny have cared for him and loved him while enduring unbelievable stress, but I know your hearts are grieving. Let's all pray that the clot won't move."

There were tears in his eyes as he left the room to give orders to Jonathan's nurse. We knew he had become very attached to Jonathan and desperately wanted to see him well.

After the doctor left the room, we realized that Jamie had disappeared. She was not in Jonathan's room or at the nurses' station. We frantically searched up and down the halls. Finally, we located her in an empty room. She had overheard the doctor's comments, and we found her crumpled on the floor crying uncontrollably.

"I don't want him to die," she sobbed.

She was almost fourteen, but we had shielded her from much of the trauma of the past year-and-a-half. She knew Jonathan was very sick, but this was the first time she had come face-to-face with the reality that he could die.

We began a tradition that evening that continues in our family today. The three of us sat in a circle on the floor in that hospital room, and one by one, took turns sharing everything in our hearts—no matter how big or how small—that we were worried about. Then we took turns praying aloud, relinquishing everything that concerned us to the Lord.

"Blessed be the God and Father of our Lord Jesus Christ, the Father of mercies and God of all comfort, who comforts us in all our tribulation" (2 Corinthians 1:3-4a). We experienced that day the comfort that we so desperately needed. God gently wrapped His arms around us and embraced us with His mercy and compassion.

Chapter 12

Snow Storms Inside and Out

Miraculously, Jonathan's blood clot did not move, but he was still not out of danger. By January 12 he had begun breathing sufficiently on his own, which allowed the doctors to remove the intubation and ventilator equipment. We were also encouraged that he seemed to be very gradually emerging from the coma.

I had always assumed that television shows accurately depicted someone emerging from a comatose state. One minute the person lay perfectly still in a coma; the next minute they miraculously appeared alert, wide-awake, and completely back to normal. Unfortunately, television is not reality. Most patients who recover from a coma slowly progress through different levels of cognitive functioning. Doctors measure improvement by observing verbal response, visual response, and motor response.

Jonathan still had not spoken a word, and his eyes, though open, did not seem to be registering his environment. His motor response, however, did show signs of improvement. He no longer lay curled in a fetal position, and he seemed to have purposeful movement. His appetite had returned, though we had to feed him. Strangely, he wanted to eat everything—broccoli, squash, cauliflower—foods that no amount of *Star Wars* toys could have bribed him to eat previously. It dawned on us sadly that he tasted nothing. Nevertheless, it was a small step forward because in spite of all the intestinal surgery he had undergone, he could successfully eat, digest, and eliminate through his ileostomy ... until January 19.

On January 19 his abdomen began to swell and there ceased to be any output into his ostomy bag. Though unable to talk, he began to moan and cry out in pain. His surgeon feared that he had developed a bowel obstruction. X-rays confirmed the diagnosis. His doctors spent most of the day running tests and attempting to come up with a non-surgical solution while Jonathan continued to suffer. I was running out of patience. Jonathan was obviously in excruciating pain, and the delay made no sense. Between tests, they explained the reason for the delay. Considering all that Jonathan had been through in the previous ten days, they simply did not feel that physically he could survive another surgery. However, they were running out of options.

His previous surgeries had caused him to form numerous adhesions—scar tissue—in his abdomen. The adhesions had formed a blockage. In order to prevent this condition from reoccurring, they made a decision to thread a tube throughout his entire digestive tract. The doctor would insert the tube into his nose, proceed down the back of his throat, and wind it through his small intestine. It would temporarily remain in place long enough to prevent adhesions from causing blockages in his small bowel. Inserting the tube required anesthesia and surgery, and we could only pray that his ravaged body would be strong enough to survive.

The anesthesiologist met with us prior to the surgery. "I need to talk with you about Jonathan's surgery," he said pulling us aside. "Surgical patients are rated on a scale of 'A,' 'B,' 'C,' 'D,' or 'F.' Almost all surgeries are rated 'A,' meaning that we fully expect a successful outcome. We wouldn't even operate on a patient rated 'F.' Jonathan is going into this surgery with a rating no higher than a 'D.' You need to know that he is considered extremely high risk. We will monitor him closely and do everything possible to keep him stable." He squeezed Johnny's arm gently and gave us a sympathetic look as he left to prep for surgery.

For the first time since Jonathan became sick, we had to wait alone during his surgery. We had spent the entire day conferring with doctors and waiting for test results, oblivious to dire weather reports echoing across metro Atlanta. We had no idea we were in the direct path of a major snow and ice storm. As the orderly wheeled Jonathan into surgery, the sleet began to fall and the temperature plummeted. The ominous clouds and the cold icy conditions outside mirrored the condition of my soul. I was bone weary, physically, mentally, emotionally, and yes, spiritually. There had been too many life-threatening crises piled one on top of each other in too short a span of time. I was beginning to lose hope.

While we sat alone in the waiting room, a phone call came for us. Apparently, a couple from our church had signed up to bring dinner to us that day. Even though it was late afternoon and we had eaten nothing all day, we assured them that we were not hungry. Besides, it would be far too dangerous for them to attempt the trip to the hospital in the middle of the ice storm.

"We insist on coming," they exclaimed in an excited voice. "Only God could have known when we signed up to bring your dinner that you would need someone who owned a jeep with 4-wheel drive." (Though they are common today, vehicles with 4-wheel drive were not commonplace in the early 1980s.) "We'll have no difficulty getting there. We want to wait with you and pray with you until the surgery is over."

Tears flooded my eyes. God was slowly beginning to teach us that even though our circumstances are often bleak, He never forsakes us. He always provides exactly what we need, exactly when we need it. This precious couple risked the storm to come and "stand in the gap" with us and pray.

Another surprise was in store for us that day. Sonny (we never knew his real name), one of the hospital pharmacists, had developed a friendship with Jonathan during Jonathan's numerous hospital stays. Sonny was young, outgoing, and as mischievous as Jonathan was. He could always bring a smile to Jonathan's face. He was heartbroken over Jonathan's decline and had been searching for a way to penetrate the mental fog that surrounded Jonathan. We entered Jonathan's ICU room to wait out his surgery and were startled to see Sonny perched precariously high up on a ladder totally engaged in hanging something from the ceiling.

"Whatever are you doing?"

"Take a look." His face glowed with fun and mischief. Our gaze moved upward. Paper snowflakes covered the ceiling. He had cut out various sizes of paper snowflakes, attached strings to each one of them, and hung them from the tiles in the ceiling with paper clips. Every time the heating system came on, the air blowing through the registers forced the paper snowflakes to sway with the breeze. They appeared to be swirling around the ceiling.

"Since Jonathan can't go out and play in the snow, I brought it inside for him!"

"I can't believe the ICU nurses gave you permission to do this," I said in amazement. The nurses had diligently protected Jonathan's environment because his immune system was at an all-time low. They had allowed no one in his room except immediate family and necessary medical personnel. Johnny, Jamie, and I were often required to wear surgical masks and gowns when we entered.

"Who said they gave me permission?" he proudly replied, grinning broadly. "I didn't ask them for permission. Sometimes you just have to do what you think is right, with or without permission." No wonder he and Jonathan had been such good buddies. Both of them had the same rebellious gene.

Jonathan barely survived the surgery. His blood pressure had dropped dangerously low before stabilizing. His surgeon did manage to weave the tube all through his digestive system to prevent any further blockages.

Jonathan continued to recover from the surgery over the following days. But it seemed that as soon as we began to relax and think that surely the worse must be over, the other shoe would fall. That happened again on January 23.

It had been necessary to restrain Jonathan's hands following the surgery to relieve the blockage because his mental status had not improved. His nurses had tied his hands to the sides of his bed with long strips of cloth. He still was unable to talk, but his eyes pleaded with us to free his hands. He constantly struggled to break free of the restraints. We did our best to explain, but it was obvious that his mind did not comprehend what we were saying. We could never leave him unattended—not even for five minutes. When the three of us left for the cafeteria, we made sure the ICU nurse remained in his room until we returned.

On January 23 we ate our evening meal together and brought each other up to date on the day's events. When we returned to Jonathan's room, full-blown chaos greeted us at the door. We had been so engrossed in our conversation with each other in the cafeteria that we had not even heard when a "code" blared over the intercom directing all available doctors to Jonathan's room "stat." A nightmare played out before our eyes. Jonathan lay in the bed with blood pouring from his nose, his hands completely freed from the restraints, and the tube that his surgeon had so painstakingly threaded throughout his entire digestive tract lay on the bed beside him. He had managed to remove almost all of the tube. The part that he had not removed had lodged in his throat, blocking his air passage and threatening to choke him.

We waited in the hall outside his room for the doctors to remove the tube. No one said a word. We were all in shock. Questions flooded our minds. Where was the nurse who was supposed to have been with him? Why had she left him alone when he was clearly a critical ICU patient? Would this be the final blow that would end Jonathan's life? Why did God continue to allow him to suffer?

The doctors finally emerged from his room. They had managed to remove the rest of the tube, but there was no way to tell the extent of the damage until they conducted tests. His doctor, usually very calm, collected, and easy-going, was angrier than I'd ever seen him. "This should never have happened, and I will personally investigate and make sure it never happens again. It's likely his small bowel has folded upon itself like an accordion. Only time will tell if he will be okay."

Once again, God performed a miracle. Amazingly, tests revealed that no permanent damage had resulted when Jonathan pulled out the tube. Everything seemed to be flowing through his digestive tract with no problems.

It wasn't that I wasn't grateful that God had once again spared Jonathan's life. I truly was. But in the span of two weeks, Jonathan had experienced a massive grand mal seizure, reverted from being completely mentally normal to being comatose, survived a blood clot, withstood surgery for an intestinal blockage, and now this. I had never experienced this level of discouragement. I had an overwhelming desire to run away—to simply get in the car and drive as far away as I could. Psalm 55:6-8 perfectly expressed the way I felt: "Oh, that I had wings like a dove! For then I would fly away and be at rest. Indeed, I would wander far off, and remain in the wilderness. I would hasten my escape from the windy storm and tempest."

I sat silently for days, staring vacantly into space, dreaming of running from the "storm and tempest." My thoughts fluctuated from picturing myself basking in the sun on a beach somewhere without a care in the world, to realizing that there was no corner of the world that I could flee to that would change our circumstances. I was grieving: grieving over a son who had not died, but was nevertheless gone; grieving over an uncertain future; and grieving spiritually over unanswered questions from my God whom I thought I knew.

And I was angry, angrier with God than I had ever been. More than once, I sat alone in the darkness and screamed at Him, "I love You, but I am so angry with You for allowing this to happen to my only son. You had the power to stop it, and You chose not to. I thought You loved Jonathan. I thought You loved our family. Is this the way You show love?"

I ranted and raved like a spoiled child because I didn't get my way. Desperate for answers, I began to study and absorb the book of Job in the Bible. Job had been a faithful servant of God's, yet God had granted Satan permission to test him. As a result, Job had lost everything—his wealth, his servants, all ten of his children, and his health. *Surely, Job was outraged with God,* I thought. Nothing could have been further from the truth. Job 1:21b-22, reveal Job's response to all that he had lost: "the Lord gave and the Lord has taken away; Blessed be the name of the Lord. In all this Job did not sin nor charge God with wrong. Job 2:10b states, "Shall we indeed accept good from God, and shall we not accept adversity?" Finally Job 13:15 acknowledges Job's steadfast faith, "Though He slay me, yet will I trust Him."

I desperately wanted and needed to trust God as totally and completely as Job had. I had been a Christian since I was eight years old, but I was still an immature Christian. It was at that lowest of low points that God began to mature me and teach me how to live an abundant, joyful life with Him, regardless of my circumstances. Micah 7:8c states: "When I sit in darkness, the Lord will be a light to me."

As I began to delve daily into His Word and search the Scriptures for answers—answers that only He could provide—I began to experience a close, personal relationship with the Creator of the universe unlike anything I had known before. I was still grieving, but I knew I did not grieve alone.

Chapter 13

Braves Mania and Financial Miracles

February brought some welcome changes. After two and a half weeks of steady improvement (and no crises) and tests showing no bowel obstructions, Jonathan progressed to clear liquids and eventually to solid food. He seemed a little apprehensive about eating initially; understandably after all he had been through. We realized his sense of taste had returned when he absolutely refused broccoli, squash, and cauliflower.

He was becoming more alert every day, but it was difficult to measure his progress. His eyes appeared brighter and more observant, but he remained non-verbal and unresponsive to commands. He continued to appear mentally a long way from where he had previously been.

As I entered the hospital one morning, I could sense immediately that something was afoot. Groups of people clustered throughout the lobby and spilled into the hallways, whispering and chatting in an excited tone. "What is going on this morning?" I inquired of the first person I encountered.

"Haven't you heard?" The man was gawking at me as though I had recently arrived from a foreign planet. "The Atlanta Braves are visiting patients today! We're hoping to get some autographs before they leave the hospital."

That would be nice, I thought, but I didn't have time to wait around hoping for a Braves spotting. I was running late, as usual, and Johnny needed to leave for work. I hurried up the elevator, made my way to the ICU area, rounded the corner near Jonathan's room, and came to a screeching halt outside his door. Hordes of people blocked the entrance to his room, craning their necks, and pushing and shoving for a better view. I elbowed my way through the mob and finally wormed my way into the crowded room. I could not believe my eyes. Several of the Atlanta Braves filled the small space in Jonathan's room and surrounded his bed. The Braves!

Two of the guys were busy signing a Braves poster and autographing a Braves t-shirt for Jonathan. Several others surrounded Jonathan's bed attempting to communicate with him. The broadcaster for the Braves had also accompanied them to Scottish Rite.

Johnny had managed to locate our camera and had begun snapping photographs as fast as his trembling fingers would allow. As amazing as it all was, I was at a loss. How had the Braves ended up in ICU in Jonathan's room? I knew that special visitors to the hospital normally did not visit ICU patients. However, Jonathan had developed a very close friendship with the head of public relations at Scottish Rite and apparently had wrapped his little arms around her heart. She had brought the Braves straight to Jonathan's room, knowing that we were struggling to find ways to stimulate Jonathan's mind.

A huge crowd of doctors, nurses, and lab technicians had gathered outside Jonathan's room, selecting that very moment to "check on" Jonathan's progress. During the previous season, the Braves had won the National League Western Division championship, making them more popular than ever. For us, it was a bittersweet moment. A few days earlier, Jonathan would have been thrilled beyond measure; the day they visited, he seemed completely unaware of their presence.

On February 4 Jonathan finally moved from ICU back to the main floor. We were excited to be back with the nurses and staff we had come to love over the past year-and-a-half. It felt like we had come home. Everyone made a fuss over Jonathan and enthusiastically welcomed him back. Though they attempted to hide it, I saw more than one tear slide down their cheeks. Jonathan had left their care on January 5 perfectly normal except for his ulcerative colitis; he had returned to their floor unable to walk or talk, mentally disabled, and with a seizure disorder.

On a brighter note, Jamie was experiencing her first year in high school, and in spite of our abnormal life, she was excelling in every area. That in itself was no small miracle. For the past year-and-a-half, it had been necessary for her to bring her homework to the hospital and attempt to complete it while surrounded by numerous diversions. She cringed at the idea of my talking to her teachers about how abnormal our life had been. Consequently, they were completely unaware of our circumstances. I had no idea that at the beginning of her freshmen year she had prayed that God would allow her to graduate four years later as the class valedictorian. That seemed like a tall order. She had always been serious about her schoolwork, but because of Jonathan's illness, her life had consisted of one interruption after another.

We watched her emerge into a beautiful young woman both inside and out right before our very eyes. While in the eighth grade, she had endured, as many eighth graders do, braces on her teeth and eyeglasses; however, she also had to wear an embarrassing back brace to correct a mild scoliosis condition. The next year she shed the back brace and the braces on her teeth, and contact lenses replaced the glasses. She emerged from her cocoon like the metamorphosis of a butterfly.

However, the most beautiful change was invisible from the outside because it occurred on the inside. Early each morning as I dressed and left my bedroom headed for the kitchen, I detected a sliver of light escaping beneath Jamie's closed door. I learned early on not to disturb her. Each morning she set her alarm to allow time for studying God's Word, taking notes on what God was teaching her, and spending time on her knees in prayer. She had no idea what an encouragement she was to Johnny and me during a time when we were struggling to make sense out of our chaotic life.

Jamie's first boyfriend arrived on the scene during her freshman year. The son of one of my closest friends, he and Jamie attended the same high school and the same church. I knew we had entered a "new" phase when he asked if he could take her out to dinner and to a movie. Since he was sixteen, and she was only fourteen, we insisted that they see each other in group settings at school or church until they were older. He often came to the hospital with Jamie in the evenings, and they worked on their homework together or spent time trying to top the most current scores on the one and only archaic video game in the hospital lobby. Jamie spent so much time at the hospital that she quickly earned the top score every time she played the game. They "dated" for two years until he left for college. I've always viewed their relationship as a gift from God that brought diversion into her life during that turbulent time, when much of our lives consisted of grief and sadness.

Our financial situation had rapidly morphed into a matter of grave concern. Health insurance during the early 80s usually involved an 80/20 plan—80% paid by the insurance company and 20% paid by the family—with a lifetime maximum that the insurance company would pay. Our hospital bills had become so monumental it was increasingly difficult to pay the 20%. All of Jonathan's doctors had graciously agreed to accept whatever the insurance company paid and not bill us for the remaining 20%, but a much bigger problem loomed ahead. Jonathan's lifetime health insurance maxed out at $300,000, and we had already used $280,000. Jonathan had almost used up his entire lifetime amount at age seven! I vacillated between praying about the situation and worrying about it. I could visualize us homeless, maybe living in a tent (a cheap tent at that) in someone's back yard with nothing to eat—not even a morsel of chocolate.

Johnny had never been a worrier, and frankly, it had started to annoy me—Big Time! "How can you not worry?" I challenged him. "We have no plan whatsoever for paying these enormous hospital bills, and there is no end in sight." Jonathan remained a long way from being well.

"Worrying," he patiently assured me, "is a waste of time and energy. God knows our needs and has promised to supply them. It will be exciting to see how He does it. I can hardly wait to see how God is going to take care of our situation!"

Did I mention that Johnny is the eternal optimist? Well, I couldn't wait either, and today wouldn't be too soon. I didn't have long to stew over our dilemma. The following week Johnny received a call at work from someone in the Human Resources department requesting an appointment. Johnny arrived on time the following day for the meeting, and after exchanging a few pleasantries, the HR director got right to the point.

"Johnny, I'm aware that your son has been critically ill for over a year, and you are close to running out of insurance for him. I will be issuing a memo to everyone in the company later in the week, but because of your unique situation, I wanted you to be the first to know. Our entire company is in the process of changing insurance carriers, and it will be effective next month. Your son will have a new lifetime maximum of $500,000 with the new company. He will be viewed by the new insurance company the same as someone who has never been sick."

WOW! Some may consider this merely a coincidence. You will never convince us. God had chosen to honor Johnny's faith that He would provide for us; and God used that experience to teach me a valuable lesson about relying on Him and not worrying.

Psalm 37:25b brings assurance: "I have not seen the righteous forsaken, nor His descendants begging bread."

As long as I live, I will never forget that beautiful miracle God provided for us at just the right time. James Dobson once said, "God is seldom early but He's never late."

Chapter 14

Laughter, Hugs, and Home to Bed

On February 9 Jonathan began physical therapy. He was still overweight, making any physical activity difficult, but his doctors were gradually tapering off his cortisone medication, and his weight had begun to drop. His physical therapist began very slowly by having him sit up in a chair and kick a large beach ball back and forth. Within a few days, he began taking short tentative steps, holding on to handrails with therapists on each side. He had not walked in over a month, and that, added to all the extensive abdominal surgery he had undergone, made walking extremely painful.

On February 14 Jonathan gave us a wonderful Valentine's Day gift. He walked for the first time without assistance. He pulled himself up from his chair and took baby steps around a physical therapy table holding on to the table all the way around.

We continued to pray for his verbal skills to return. One day in early February, while I was taking him for a stroll in his wheelchair, he began making sputtering noises. I stopped and knelt down in front of him and attempted to repeat the sounds he had made. He rewarded me with a treat. He began to laugh every time I mimicked his noises. We had not heard his laughter in months. He laughed so hard he shook all over—deep belly laughs. I wanted to jump up and down and dance down the hall. I grabbed the handles of his wheelchair, sprinted hurriedly down the hall, and rushed him back to his room, summoning his nurses to come and witness this miracle.

A few days later he finally began to talk. It happened on a Saturday in February while I caught up on housework and Johnny kept vigil at the hospital. The nurses had completed Jonathan's morning bath, changed his bed sheets, and administered his oral and IV medications, leaving him to rest. Instead of resting, he seemed extremely agitated and frustrated.

"What seems to be the problem, buddy?" Johnny asked, never expecting a reply. Slowly and barely above a whisper Jonathan began to utter his first tentative words.

"Why don't you teach me how to ..." The last word faded from his lips not discernable, but it didn't matter. After five long weeks, he had talked. Jamie and I rushed to the hospital, and he rewarded us with more words, "mom," "hug," and a phrase that brought tears to our eyes, "home to bed." Over the next few days, his vocabulary increased. He added "daddy," "Jamie," and "I love you." He had always loved music and he began to sing. He serenaded us with favorite songs from his past: "Old McDonald," "Row, Row, Row Your Boat," and "Jesus Loves Me." He sang them over and over creating beautiful music to our ears.

One afternoon Jonathan sat beside his doctor dangling his legs off the side of the bed during an exam. Suddenly, Jonathan stretched out his small arms toward the doctor, as though he wanted a hug. Obligingly, the doctor enveloped him in a huge bear hug. As they sat there side by side, Jonathan looked up at him and whispered, "I'm better; I'm better." Even Jonathan's stoic doctor reveled in the tender moment.

Jonathan continued to experience mild seizures. His neurologist increased his medication and ordered another EEG. Pleased with the return of some elementary verbal skills, I commented to the neurologist that at least he had finally progressed beyond the baby stage that had described his behavior for so long. His reply totally shocked me. "He was not even at the baby stage a few weeks ago. He was more like a fetus." The EEG revealed minimal seizure activity and much improved brain activity over the previous EEG. Good news that we desperately needed to hear.

We finally received the best news of all: He was going home. Though excited about regaining some semblance of normalcy in our lives, for the first time in eighteen months, fear gripped my heart at the thought of leaving the security of the hospital. Marsha, his nurse, and I sat down together a few days before his release to discuss his home care. It was daunting to say the least. I secretly entertained thoughts that when he returned to his home environment and experienced a familiar setting he would quickly regain mentally what he had lost.

The first month at home was exhausting physically and emotionally for all of us. Not only did he not seem to improve, in some areas, he seemed to have regressed. Though he had previously been able to verbalize "mom," "dad," and "Jamie," somewhere along the way that ability had vanished completely. He began to refer to all three of us as "person," and it quickly became all too apparent that he did not have a clue who we were. We watched him regress physically as well. His eating and drinking dwindled daily leaving him weak and lethargic. No amount of coaxing worked.

The end of March found him back in the hospital, severely dehydrated. Since he was not eating enough to maintain his nutritional needs, his doctors made the decision to begin home IV therapy. A home health service arranged to deliver hyperalimination (IV feeding) to our home each week. We would need two IV machines in his bedroom to supply his complete daily nutritional needs: one to provide his daily feedings, and one to supply necessary lipids, or fats, that the body requires. He still had a central-line catheter, so, thankfully, we would not have to stick him with needles. We simply connected the plastic tubing to his catheter each night at bedtime and "fed" him overnight.

In addition to nightly IV feedings, he wore diapers, had an ileostomy bag that his bowel fluids emptied into, continued to experience seizures, consumed tons of medication that had to be administered at various intervals throughout the day, and his central-line catheter had to be kept sterile at all times. (We donned sterile masks, gloves, and gowns every time we changed the dressing.) We also daily had to record for his doctors his urine and ileostomy output, perform tests on his urine, conduct tests on any rectal drainage to check for the presence of blood, change his catheter dressing every three days using sterile technique, and weigh him once a week. I dared anyone to ask me what I did in my spare time. At one time my heart's desire had been to be a nurse, but if this was an example of God's sense of humor, I wasn't laughing. I was terrified that I wasn't up to the task.

Chapter 15

Mother's Day Emergency and Surprise Retreat

We settled into a routine of sorts. Johnny went to work, Jamie went to school, and I spent every waking moment caring for Jonathan. Despondency settled over me like a deep, dark cloud. Every situation screamed how abnormal our existence had become.

My neighbor casually mentioned one day that she would be taking her boys to ball practice and Cub Scouts. I could hardly hold back the tears. Jonathan should have been participating in those same activities; yet, our activities consisted of doctor visits and trips to the hospital. I knew wallowing in pity would accomplish nothing, but I didn't care.

To make matters worse, since Jonathan had lost all the extra weight he had gained from the medications and was getting adequate nutrition through the IV feedings, he had gone from lethargic to hyperactive. He raced through the house at neck-breaking speed, turned the faucets on and off, bounced up and down on his bed as though it were a trampoline, emphatically slammed the door every time he entered or exited a room, shouted angrily at no one in particular, and threw toys and other objects forcefully across the room. I seriously considered booking a reservation for myself at the local mental hospital.

Jonathan's gastro doctor suggested we see a psychiatrist. I wasn't sure if he meant for Jonathan or me. We both definitely needed some help. We scheduled an appointment for early April and looked forward to hearing the psychiatrist suggestions.

On the day of Jonathan's appointment, we sat anxiously in the waiting room. The lights in the room glowed softly, and music played quietly in the background, providing a calm, serene atmosphere. I had never been in a psychiatrist's office before, and the temptation to steal furtive peeks at the other patients was powerful. My imagination over their prospective dilemmas shifted to overdrive. Suddenly, the nurse called Jonathan's name, and the reality of our own situation moved to the forefront. Johnny and I stood to accompany Jonathan into the doctor's office. "No, no, no," the nurse pronounced, vigorously shaking her index finger back and forth at us. "The doctor wants to see Jonathan ... alone."

As the two of them disappeared through the door, Johnny and I stole a grin at each other. We glanced at our watches. "I'll give her five minutes, max." Johnny wagered.

"I don't think she'll make it three minutes," I countered.

Sure enough, within five minutes the nurse came tearing through the door wearing a look of desperation. "The doctor needs to see you immediately!" she yelled in a panicky voice. She rapidly motioned for us to follow her into the doctor's office.

Johnny and I secretly enjoyed a "told you so" moment and stifled a giggle as she led us down the long hallway. As we entered the doctor's spacious office, the entire scenario struck me as strange. The middle-aged psychiatrist, casually dressed in a skirt and blouse, sat barefoot in an over-stuffed chair with her feet tucked up under her. She randomly leafed through Jonathan's file while Jonathan raced around her office like a runaway train. The thought occurred to me that maybe we had come to the wrong place for help. We quickly gave her a condensed version of Jonathan's medical history. "The main reason we are here," I explained, "is to find out what we need to do to get him back to his original level of functioning mentally, and emotionally."

Her answer stunned us. "We must assume there has been some permanent brain damage, and he will never return to his previous level of functioning." She delivered her verdict as casually and matter-of-factly as if she were stating her restaurant preference for the evening meal. The reality of Jonathan's future stretched out before us with that one condemning sentence.

I didn't hear anything else she said throughout the remainder of the appointment. I could feel the blood draining from my head, and I felt dizzy and faint. I silently begged God to get me out of there before I passed out from lack of oxygen. No one up to that point had even hinted that his current mental state would be permanent. The neurologist had continued to tell us that his neurological problems were a result of all the cortisone medication he had taken for almost two years and his poor health in general. He seemed to think that as he improved nutritionally and medically, his mental state would return to normal.

We were both quiet the entire trip home. The psychiatrist's assessment had left us both drained and in shock. We sat down with Jamie when she came home from school and related the psychiatrist's report. "Regardless of what happens," I said, "we will continue to love Jonathan and care for him, and we will attempt to make our lives as normal as possible. We will never hide him away in an institution or be ashamed or embarrassed by his behavior." (I would eat those words many, many times!)

I felt that it was necessary to relate to Jamie exactly what the psychiatrist had said, but in my heart, I didn't believe for one minute that his condition was permanent. I simply chose not to believe it. In order to preserve my own sanity, I had to believe his condition was temporary. We had spent hours on our knees praying for his healing, and people we had never even met from around the world were praying for him. Surely God would honor those prayers.

At a follow-up appointment with the psychiatrist, she discussed ways to get Jonathan to eat and drink so that we could discontinue his IV feedings. She also suggested we see a behavioral psychologist and a speech pathologist to try to resolve at least some of his issues.

Before we could see either, we faced another emergency. Jonathan had been taking a blood thinner since his previous blood clot. Even though we went to the hospital weekly to check the level of blood thinner in his system, the medication had become too elevated. Ironically, on Mother's Day, he began to bleed profusely. By the time we arrived at the emergency room, he was passing huge clots of blood from the rectal area. His lips were not even discernable on his pale face. We had called to alert the doctors that we were on the way. The ER doctor immediately went into action. He shouted orders at the nurses and loudly reprimanded them for not moving quickly enough.

The room came alive with activity. A nurse quickly started giving Jonathan a blood transfusion, and the color gradually returned to his face. When he finally stabilized medically, the doctor took us aside. He apologized for his behavior in the emergency room. "I hope you understand," he explained. "We had to act very quickly. Jonathan had already gone into shock from loss of blood, and we were losing him rapidly. I could actually feel him slipping away. We did not have a minute to spare."

They later discovered that Jonathan's emergency had resulted from an infection in his blood stream. He remained in the hospital for another two weeks.

Surprisingly, the behavioral psychologist scheduled a visit to evaluate him in the hospital. A primary concern involved his refusal to eat. Her diagnosis of anorexia shocked us to the core. She explained that often lack of control in one's life manifested itself in anorexia. Jonathan had lost so much in such a short period. Most of what he had suffered, he had had no control over;

however, he could control whether or not he would eat. And he chose not to.

His reasoning ability seemed so limited that I wasn't totally convinced that he could think through that process and come to that conclusion. He had experienced so much abdominal pain, I thought perhaps he associated the pain with eating and had decided not to eat. Whatever the reason, the behavioral psychologist tried several different techniques, and Jonathan actually began to eat a small amount of food for the first time in weeks. He still required the IV feedings at home, but at least we were beginning to see improvement.

She also agreed with the psychiatrist that he desperately needed speech therapy. She arranged for Jonathan to see a speech pathologist on staff at Scottish Rite. "Before I leave I have a prescription that you need to act on immediately." I assumed she had written a prescription to increase his appetite. Reading it brought a smile to my face. It wasn't for Jonathan at all. It was a prescription for Johnny and me. The RX simply stated:

One week in Florida … Alone!!

I appreciated the thought though it was completely unrealistic. She, however, could not have been more serious. She demanded that we give her a report of our vacation plans at Jonathan's next appointment.

We certainly wanted and needed to get away, but we were barely holding our heads above water financially. Every dime we had went for medical expenses not covered by insurance. We simply could not afford a week in Florida, or anywhere else for that matter, let alone the expense for a nurse to stay with Jonathan twenty-four hours a day while we frolicked on the beach. In addition, Jonathan remained so fragile medically that I emotionally could not have left him for that long. She would just have to accept the reality of our situation.

An interesting piece of mail came shortly thereafter. Addressed to Johnny and me from our friends and co-workers, the enclosed note read:

> *"We realize your family has been under tremendous stress for the past two years. We want to do something to help. We came up with a plan that we thought you might enjoy. We have arranged for the two of you to have a weekend at our expense at a resort hotel at Lake Lanier, just a few miles north of Atlanta.*
>
> *We have also arranged for Jonathan's favorite nurses, Marsha and Lisel, to stay with him around the clock while you're away. Hopefully, Jamie can stay with a friend and the two of you can have a relaxing, stress-free weekend away."*

My eyes welled up with tears as God reminded me once again of His goodness. He knew how desperately we needed a respite from the raging tempest that had swirled around us for so long; and He used those precious friends to supply it.

Chapter 16

Runaway

T he behavioral psychologist asked me to list every area I could think of that we needed to work on. I suppressed a chuckle when I realized she wasn't joking. I thought the lengthy catalog of grievances I handed to her would probably convince her to send us packing. She perused the list and then politely suggested that we focus on one or two of the most severe behaviors to begin with and later address the others. Jonathan's propensity for running away had definitely risen to the top of the list because of the danger it posed. I shared with her how serious the problem had become.

One Saturday Johnny, the children, and I had gone shopping at a local Christian bookstore. While we were checking out the latest books and tapes, we thought we had a firm grip on Jonathan's hand. Suddenly, he broke free from our grasp and began racing with the speed of lightning up and down the aisles, rounding corners at an astonishing pace. He could put an Olympic athlete to shame. Jamie bolted after him down the Bible aisle, Johnny headed for the tapes and records section, and I scrambled towards the cards and stationary display. Customers ceased their shopping and stared with looks of total disbelief at the four of us flying through the store. Their mouths were unconsciously gaping open. Jamie finally headed Jonathan off at the pass (i.e. the children's section), where we apprehended him, marched him to the car, and corralled him in the back seat.

Another time Jamie and I had taken him with us to a fabric store. We were congratulating ourselves that we had managed to locate our purchases and get them to the checkout counter with no mishaps. Unfortunately, we had to wait in line behind several customers. I plopped Jonathan up on the counter while we waited so he wouldn't run away. Even though he was small for his age, it probably did look a bit unusual for him to be sitting there since he was seven years old. The sales clerk glared at us and said indignantly, "He can't sit up there. We don't allow anyone to sit on the counter. He has to get down right now!"

"Trust me, ma'am," I said, trying to stay calm, "you don't want me to put him down."

"No one is allowed to sit on the counter," she screeched, her voice growing louder by the minute. "Tell him to get down right now."

"Okay, if you insist," I said. The clerk was really starting to annoy me, and I have to admit I didn't try very hard to restrain Jonathan. Down he went, legs flying and arms flapping like a chicken. He flew like a runaway train. By the time we caught him, bolts of fabric, packets of buttons, and rolls of ribbon lay in his path of destruction. Needless to say, Jamie and I have never been able to return to that store since that day without wearing some sort of disguise.

The most frightening situation occurred at home. Jamie was away at church camp, and Jonathan and I were taking advantage of a beautiful summer day, throwing a ball back and forth in the backyard. A four-foot high chain-link fence enclosed our entire backyard, providing, we thought, a safe place for Jonathan to release some energy. As an additional precaution, we had tied a length of rope around the gate latch making it impossible for him to open the gate. Before I realized what was happening, I caught a glimpse out of the corner of my eye of a fast moving object streaking past me and heading straight for the street. We had no idea Jonathan could climb *over* the fence! Unfortunately, not being as agile as he was, I could not scale the fence as easily as he had. Sheer terror filled my mind as I struggled to loosen the rope we had tied around the latch. I screamed for him to stop running, even as I heard a car coming over the hill in front of our house. By the time I managed to open the gate, I was afraid to look at what must surely be a tragedy. When I finally arrived at the scene, I could hardly believe what had happened.

Sina, my next-door neighbor, had come out her front door to collect her mail just in time to see Jonathan flying across the front yard. She ran after him and caught him seconds before the car came barreling down the road in front of our house. Visibly shaken, the driver had stopped, realizing that she had been seconds away from hitting a child. Sina, almost in tears over the near disaster, sank to the ground. I was furious. We had spent every waking moment for the past two years struggling to keep Jonathan alive, only to have him almost killed by running in front of a car. I jerked him inside none too gently, shouting all the while that a car had almost hit him. He just stared at me with those big brown eyes totally clueless as to why I was so upset.

As I related all this to the behavioral psychologist, she formulated a plan that we could only pray would be successful. The psychologist and I began taking Jonathan to a small strip shopping center near her office. She and I would stand several feet apart on the sidewalk, each of us clutching a handful of colorful pieces of candy. Jonathan loved candy, so the plan involved having him walk—not run—back and forth between the two of us. Each time he walked to one of us, we rewarded him with a few pieces of candy. If he ran, he received no reward. I was skeptical about this working, but I certainly didn't have a better plan. Johnny, Jamie, and I also practiced this technique at home, and gradually Jonathan did improve. It took several years and several more frightening episodes, however, before we completely conquered his inclination to run away.

Chapter 17

Searching for Answers

W e loved Jonathan's speech pathologist the moment we met her in July of 1983. Tall and thin with beautiful auburn hair, she manifested an air of elegance. Gentle and soft-spoken, she connected with Jonathan from the beginning. Her eyes filled with tears as we related his story.

We arrived at her office, located in a wing of Scottish Rite Hospital, for his first appointment with a considerable amount of anticipation. I was pleased to discover that the therapy room had a separate parents' observation room equipped with a two-way mirror. I could observe his therapy unnoticed by him. After a few therapy sessions, we read his first progress report with mixed feelings:

Jonathan presents himself as a challenging, active, difficult to test child with impaired language skills, memory, and academic skills. His personality has also been altered. Over the past several months, Jonathan has made very good progress in the areas of comprehension and non-verbal skills. He is able to follow selected one-step commands and several two-step commands, (i.e. Pick up the ball and put it on the table.) Much of his spontaneous language has become more appropriate. For example, on one occasion he pointed to a music box and said, "Crank it up." He continues to exhibit a great deal of difficulty naming people and objects. His behavior, characterized by shouting, hitting, and throwing objects, is felt to interfere with his progress. It is difficult to determine if his negative behavior is a residual component of some neurological damage or an emotional reaction to his condition. However, if this anger can be appropriately channeled, progress should be able to be made at a faster rate.

His therapy sessions often left me totally drained emotionally. I could barely tolerate watching his lack of cooperation and erratic behavior. I would leave the observation room crying and so distraught that his therapist recommended that I only observe him occasionally. "Use his time in therapy to read a book or take a walk. Do something you enjoy." It sounded like good advice to me.

Jonathan had become increasingly more hostile and angry with everyone. "I hate you!" and "You're dumb and stupid!" were his favorite phrases. The behavioral psychologist attempted to help us understand. "He knows that he has lost something major, though he is not able to mentally sort it all out. That is probably what's causing his hostility and depression. Oftentimes, a stroke victim who has never uttered a curse word will fill his vocabulary with unacceptable and inappropriate words. 'I hate you' and 'You're dumb and stupid' are Jonathan's curse words, so to speak." We were very thankful he wasn't old enough to know any true curse words.

Jonathan's behavior made life at home very difficult. He continued to refer to Johnny, Jamie, and me as "person." He didn't just say it passively either; he yelled with an enormous amount of hostility in his voice, "Come here, Person!" That was more difficult to accept in some ways than his medical problems. I'm convinced he had no idea who we were. He seemed lost and frightened and at the same time was fighting desperately for survival. We had to physically hold him down and restrain him just to change his diaper or empty his ileostomy bag. He reminded me of a pitiful animal who had been so severely mistreated he had no trust of anyone. Jonathan simply wanted everyone to leave him alone; and we wanted desperately to find some way to let him know how much we loved and missed the Jonathan that we had once known.

Johnny, Jamie, and I continued to pray and search the Bible for answers. I began an intense Bible study on healing. I had so many questions that seemed to have no answers:

"Why would God allow an innocent child to suffer?"

"Why doesn't He respond to our prayers for Jonathan's healing?"

"Why does He heal some but not others?"

"Is it God's will for Jonathan to be so sick?"

I struggled with these tough questions. I trusted God completely with my eternal salvation, but I also had to be able to trust Him with Jonathan. I tried to squeeze out precious time daily to study the Scriptures. As I studied, God began to reveal more and more truths from His Word.

I knew that He loved Jonathan even more than I did. Romans 8:38-39 promises: "Neither death nor life, nor angels nor principalities nor powers, nor things present nor things to come, nor height nor depth, nor any other created thing, shall be able to separate us from the love of God which is in Christ Jesus our Lord."

I formed a mental picture of Jonathan sitting in Jesus' lap with his arms wrapped tightly around Jesus' neck, both smiling broadly. I learned from God's Word that God sees our grief and trouble. "But You have seen it, for You observe trouble and grief, …" (Psalm 10:14a). However, He is under no obligation to reveal His reasons for what He allows in our lives. In fact, God never revealed to Job the reason for his suffering.

Isaiah 55:8-9 states: "For My thoughts are not your thoughts, Nor are your ways My ways, says the Lord. For as the heavens are higher than the earth, So are My ways higher than your ways, and My thoughts than your thoughts."

He is God, and what He desires most is our trust and obedience regardless of our circumstances. Distressed and overwhelmed, the writer of Psalm 77 appears convinced that God has forsaken him. He records the following thoughts in verses 7-9: "Will the Lord cast off forever? And will He be favorable no more? Has His mercy ceased forever? Has His promise failed forevermore? Has God forgotten to be gracious? Has He in anger shut up His tender mercies? "

Psalm 77:10b-13 records the Psalmist's response: "I will remember the years of the right hand of the Most High. I will remember the works of the Lord; surely I will remember Your wonders of old. I will also meditate on all Your work, and talk of Your deeds. Your way, O God, is in the sanctuary; Who is so great a God as our God?"

The Psalmist's answer to his personal distress was to remember and meditate on what God had done for him in the past and to talk to others about the greatness and awesomeness of the God that we serve.

The Bible reveals in Jeremiah 30:15 and Galatians 6:7 that often our suffering is a result of our own sin and disobedience: "Why do you cry about your affliction? Your sorrow is incurable. Because of the multitude of your iniquities, because your sins have increased, I have done these things to you" (Jeremiah 30:15). "Do not be deceived, God is not mocked; for whatever a man sows, that will he also reap" (Galatians 6:7).

Johnny and I both searched our hearts and knew that although we had certainly sinned, our goal had always been to please God and serve Him faithfully. Violating God's laws, however, is not always the reason for our suffering.

John 9:1-7 tells the story of Jesus and his disciples encountering a man who had been blind from birth. Jesus' disciples asked whether the man's blindness was a result of the blind man's sin or the sin of the man's parents. Jesus' answer in verse 3 was profound: "Neither this man nor his parents sinned, but that the works of God should be revealed in him."

Though it is often a difficult pill for us to swallow, sometimes the reason for our suffering is to glorify God in the midst of our suffering and as a result, draw people to Him.

The book of Genesis records how God allowed tremendous suffering in Joseph's life in order to mature him spiritually for the task ahead.

Psalm 119:67 reveals another possible reason for our physical pain on this earth. "Before I was afflicted I went astray, but now I keep your word." That in itself motivated me to be more obedient to God's Word.

I found enormous comfort in God's Word as I continued to study. Jeremiah 29:11-14a became a favorite passage: "For I know the thoughts that I think toward you, says the Lord, thoughts of peace and not of evil, to give you a future and a hope. Then you will call upon Me and go and pray to Me, and I will listen to you. And you will seek Me and find Me when you search for Me with all your heart. I will be found by you, says the Lord ..."

Psalm 34:18 became a favorite verse: "The Lord is near to those who have a broken heart ..."

Psalm 147:3: "He heals the brokenhearted and binds up their wounds."

As I searched the Scriptures for answers, my faith began to grow. I began to trust God with Jonathan more and more each day. I looked forward to spending time studying God's Word daily. Somewhere along the way, I ceased to be concerned with "why," though I know God understands our questioning when we're hurting deeply. Even Jesus, Himself, asked "why" from the cross when He asked God, His Father, "Why have You forsaken Me?" (Matthew 27:46b). My focus gradually shifted from anger and hopelessness to, "how can we glorify God in our situation, and what good can come from this experience?" Romans 8:28 states, "And we know that all things work together for good to those who love God, to those who are the called according to His purpose."

I began to realize that if God had permitted these circumstances in our lives, He had a purpose that would ultimately work out for His good. I desperately needed to find God's purpose so that Jonathan's suffering would not be in vain.

Chapter 18

Beware of Flying Grapes

L ife at home continued to be chaotic. Bedtime in particular had become a nightmare. Jonathan remained on IV feeding therapy, which we administered overnight every night. The only time he remained calm and still for an extended period was while he slept. Each night we connected the plastic tubing that ran between his central-line catheter and the IV machines, set the controls, turned out the light, and quietly tiptoed out of the room. Night after night within five minutes, we heard his bed creaking and the glass, fluid-filled bottles of IV feeding clanging against each other, threatening to topple over, or break and spill IV fluids everywhere. Each night we ran back into his room and found him attempting to escape his prison of plastic tubes. The only solution we found that worked consistently involved one of us lying down with him until he fell asleep. We all took turns, including Jamie, but that horrible arrangement only served to rob the three of us of precious time together each evening.

One day while talking on the phone with Marsha, his nurse from Scottish Rite, who had called to see how we were getting along, I groaned about our nighttime dilemma and asked her to pray with us for a solution. "There must be a more workable solution to this problem," I lamented.

"I know just what you need," she offered. "You need a posey."

"What in the world is a posey?" I questioned. She described the posey as a vest made out of thick canvas-like material that had two very long extensions, similar to extra long apron strings. You slipped the vest on the patient then wrapped the extensions around his waist crisscrossing them in the front. The patient (or maybe I should say the victim) was totally secure once the ends of the extensions were tied to the bedposts. If tied loosely enough, the patient could even roll from side to side, but he couldn't get up. It sounded like a dream come true to us. We practically broke the speed barrier getting to the medical supply store to buy a posey. It worked great. We literally tied Jonathan to the bed each night until he fell asleep. If a social worker had seen that arrangement, she probably would have arrested us and hauled us off to jail, but thankfully, that never happened. The vest did not hurt Jonathan in any way, and it prevented him from getting out of bed. He always fell asleep quickly when he realized he couldn't get up. Before we went to bed, we tiptoed into his room and carefully removed the posey so that he never slept all night with it on. Amazingly, he never woke up when we removed it. (We were always careful to take it off before we went to bed in the event an emergency occurred that necessitated getting him out of bed quickly.)

Grocery shopping became a major challenge. Most of the time I shopped after Jamie came home from school or Johnny from work so I could go alone. Occasionally busy schedules forced me to take Jonathan with me. Because of his hyperactivity, holding on to him and trying to shop at the same time required supernatural skills. One particular day when I took him with me stands out vividly in my memory. I decided to put him inside the grocery cart. Too big to fit in the cart where babies sit, I heaved him up into the large section of the cart along with the food I had purchased. Much to my dismay, it was like throwing Brer Rabbit into the briar patch. He began prying open all the soda cans, unraveling toilet paper, and throwing grapes at unsuspecting shoppers. To add insult to injury, I overheard a little boy shopping with his mom yell loudly enough for people two stores away to hear, "Mom, look at that big kid riding in the cart. What's wrong with him? Why can't I ride like that?" Often we didn't know whether to laugh or to cry.

One evening I strolled through the grocery store shopping alone (which I always did following the grape throwing fiasco) when I spotted Vivian, a friend of mine from church. I had spent so much time alone with Jonathan that the thought of seeing a friend and engaging in some adult conversation brought a smile to my face. We chatted for a while and she, naturally, asked about Jonathan. She had a son Jonathan's age, and he and Jonathan had previously played together often. I began to spout off my standard response: "Oh, he's gradually getting better. He's doing great. He's ..." Suddenly I stopped in mid-sentence. Over the previous months, I had become an expert at hiding my tears and pretending to smile. I'm not sure exactly what happened that day, but somehow I faced the reality of our life as I never had before. "Vivian, the truth is, Jonathan has brain damage and it's probably permanent. We're going to therapy almost every day, but his doctors aren't sure how much he will regain. I think I've lost my little boy." My eyes and heart had been like shutters tightly closed against a raging storm. Suddenly, the doors burst open wide, allowing the light of reality to pour in. The mask fell away, exposing my vulnerable heart for all to see. Tears coursed down my cheeks, smearing makeup and fogging my glasses, and I didn't even care. I felt liberated. For the first time, I had admitted to myself that Jonathan was permanently mentally disabled. And it was okay.

Frequently, when a family has an on-going crisis, friends conclude each phone call with, "let us know if we can do anything to help." They certainly mean well, and I have been guilty of repeating that phrase more than once myself. The problem with that phrase, however, is that most people who desperately need help would never ask even a close friend for assistance. My friend, Jane, was unique. She called about once a week, and instead of saying, "let me know if I can do anything to help," she always said, " I have some extra time today, and I'll be over in a few minutes to help you with whatever you need to get done." And she proved true to her word. She washed clothes, ironed, cleaned house, and helped with anything else I needed done.

Johnny and I both have birthdays in August. Jane called about halfway between Johnny's birthday and mine. "You two need to go out to dinner alone and celebrate your birthdays. I'm coming over Saturday night to stay with Jonathan and Jamie. What time would you like me to be there?" She refused to take "no" for an answer.

I had never left Jonathan before except with Marsha or Lisel, his nurses, but I felt confident Jane could handle any situation that might arise. Jamie would be at home with her, and Jamie knew almost as much about Jonathan's care as we did. We made dinner reservations and eagerly awaited our "date." I felt as giddy as a teenage girl awaiting her first prom. An entire evening out—just Johnny and me. It seemed too good to be true.

Saturday arrived, and we gave Jane a "crash" course on how to empty Jonathan's ostomy bag, what to do in case of a seizure, and how to give him his medications. We gave her the phone number of the restaurant where we planned to eat and made her promise to call us if she had any problems. (Unfortunately, in 1983 cell phones were not yet in use.)

We headed out the door. God had provided us with a beautiful starlit summer evening. Johnny rushed around and opened the car door for me and our date began. We had a wonderful time. Johnny had made reservations at an up-scale restaurant that played soft romantic music in the background. He had even arranged to have a flaming dessert brought to our table. We checked with our waiter several times, and he assured us we had not received any phone calls. We drove home relaxed and confident that Jane and Jamie had everything on the home front under control.

We were somewhat surprised that Jonathan didn't fly down the stairs to greet us at the door when he heard the garage door open—his usual custom. In fact, we didn't see him anywhere. The euphoria of the evening rapidly melted away. Panic had officially set in when Jamie finally came to the door grinning from ear to ear. "Where is Jonathan?" I asked with trepidation. "Is he alright?"

"Oh, yeah, he's fine now. They're in the bathroom."

I raced down the hall to the bathroom and found Jonathan happily playing in the tub while Jane sang to him and entertained him. "I'm sorry, Jane. You didn't have to bathe him. I would have done that later."

Jane laughed as she responded, "We had one small problem but we took care of it." It seemed that while we were away, Jonathan had managed to completely remove his ostomy bag, causing bowel fluid to seep out uncontrolled. It had not occurred to me to show Jane how to attach his bag so she had improvised by placing him in the bathtub until we returned. "I could have called and asked you to come home, but you needed an evening out, and I knew this was not a medical emergency."

The Bible says in Proverbs 18:24b: "There is a friend who sticks closer than a brother." Jane is that kind of friend.

Chapter 19

Back to School

It was time for us to make plans for Jonathan's return to school. He should have been getting ready to enter second grade, but now that was out of the question. I knew absolutely nothing about special education. Zero. I'm ashamed to say I didn't even know anyone who had a handicapped child. Jamie and Jonathan had always registered at our neighborhood school and shown up on the first day like everyone else. Jonathan's psychologist suggested I call the county office and explain what had happened to him and let them take it from there.

I located the correct number in the telephone book and asked to speak to someone in charge of special education placement. When I related our situation, her response threw me for a loop. "I want to know why he hasn't been in school for the last year!" the woman on the other end of the line barked into the phone. I thought I had explained Jonathan's medical problems adequately, but apparently she wasn't listening or according to her thinking, even a child on his deathbed belonged in school. Feeling like a delinquent parent sent to the principal's office, I tried to sound calmer than I felt.

"Ma'am, Jonathan spent most of last year in the hospital critically ill. We primarily focused on trying to keep him alive."

She informed me that the first step to registering for special education involved scheduling Jonathan for a series of tests to evaluate exactly where he placed mentally. We made an appointment to have him evaluated for placement on June 2, 1983.

The meeting to evaluate him filled me with apprehension. To put a formal label on my child that would identify him as mentally deficient for the rest of his life was unbearable and unthinkable. Thankfully, the diagnostician who conducted the evaluation proved to be understanding and genuinely concerned about Jonathan's correct placement. She assured us that because he continued to improve slowly, the committee would delay making a final decision until fall.

Summer flew by too quickly. We received notice that the meeting to decide Jonathan's placement would take place on August 25. I had prayed all summer that God would give wisdom to everyone involved in deciding where he would attend school, the type of class best suited for him, and especially the teacher assigned to him. We arrived early at the elementary school located on the other side of the county from where we lived. Jonathan's speech pathologist had agreed to attend the meeting and share her recommendations with the committee.

We located the room and were surprised when we opened the door to a room full of people. I quickly scanned the assemblage that included Kathy, Jonathan's prospective special-education teacher, the school principal, the diagnostician, a school speech pathologist, and several people from the county office. Was this really necessary to place one little boy in school? It was very intimidating to say the least.

Martha, a brave friend of ours who lived near the school, had agreed to meet us at the school and sit with Jonathan during the meeting. However, once we arrived, the committee decided it would be helpful to send Jonathan to the class they were considering for his placement. I could feel the beginnings of a migraine. Visions of the fabric store, the Christian bookstore, and the grocery store fiascos fought for attention in my brain. Thankfully, Martha volunteered to accompany him to the class and stay with him. Since Kathy, his prospective teacher, needed to attend the meeting, the principal had placed another special-ed teacher in her class.

The meeting began. Johnny and I gave a summary of Jonathan's previous two years and explained his language difficulties and his hyperactive behavior as honestly as possible. We detailed his ongoing medical challenges. We explained that we had no way of knowing how much he would regain mentally, and that though he continued to relearn, his behavior severely hampered his progress. After much discussion, the committee decided to place him in Kathy's class, a health-impaired special education class. He would attend only two hours a day initially and increase the time as we felt he could tolerate it. I would drive him to school until his school day was long enough to merit sending a bus.

I preferred delaying a long bus ride until he became more medically stable, so that decision met with our approval. In addition, the school was located about halfway between our house and Scottish Rite Hospital. We scheduled his two hours at school to end in time for me to drive him from school to his therapy sessions.

The meeting was winding down. We were nearly home free, and I could feel myself slowly beginning to exhale. Suddenly, the door burst open, and the teacher assigned to Kathy's class came charging in the room obviously agitated. She yelled loudly enough that all conversation in the room ceased. "Jonathan has been in my classroom less than two hours, and he has managed to completely disrupt the entire class. He is completely uncooperative. He refuses to do anything I ask him to do, and he has called everyone in the class 'dumb' and 'stupid.' I felt that you should know this since you're making a decision about his placement."

A hushed stillness settled over the room like a thick blanket. My lungs begged for air. It became so quiet you could hear a pin drop. I wanted to crawl under the table and hide. I could feel the heat from embarrassment creep up my neck and threaten to suffocate me. I mentally informed the Lord that this would be an excellent time for the rapture to occur.

The principal quickly broke the silence. He looked the tattletale teacher squarely in the eye and calmly informed her, "We have discussed Jonathan's behavior at length, and this is exactly what we would have expected from him." Wow! I could hardly believe my ears. I crawled out from under the table and had an overwhelming desire to hug this wonderful man for his positive attitude. Maybe Jonathan would survive school after all.

August 31, Jonathan's first day to attend school, rolled around too quickly. We had asked everyone we knew to pray for this new beginning. I clearly sensed God's presence as I drove him to school that first day. There were only six other students in his class, and most occupied wheelchairs. I quickly determined from their conversation that all the students functioned at a higher mental capacity than Jonathan. After introducing me to Jonathan's new classmates, Kathy said that she would like to try working with Jonathan without me in the room. He needed to develop independence and gradually break his strong attachment to me. She suggested I wait in the teacher's lounge, and she promised to come for me if any problems arose. Her positive, enthusiastic attitude stirred hope deep in my heart.

I had brought a book with me, but my ability to concentrate flew out the window. I decided since I had the lounge all to myself that I would spend the time praying for Jonathan. I asked God specifically to give him a positive day, and to allow something good to happen that we could remember.

Not long after I prayed, Kathy opened the door to the lounge. "I just wanted you to know Jonathan has completed a finger-painting project and has been sitting in his chair nicely. We haven't encountered any problems."

Later, his school speech pathologist came in and shared, "I don't want Jonathan to see you, but I want you to see what he's doing." I cautiously asked, "Is it something he's supposed to be doing?" I was clearly gun-shy.

"Oh yes," she replied with a smile. I peeked out the door and there he was, riding a tricycle up and down the hall, thoroughly enjoying himself. Kathy raced to keep up with him. Her attempt to give him an outlet for his vast supply of energy couldn't have made Jonathan any happier. Overall, his first day had been a success, a good beginning. A new chapter had begun in our lives.

Unfortunately, Jonathan attended school only four days before he landed back in the hospital. We had planned to visit Johnny's parents Labor Day weekend, but as we were packing to leave, Jonathan began vomiting uncontrollably. Nothing his doctors had previously prescribed seemed to help. We found ourselves once again back in the hospital. We prayed that it was only a virus; unfortunately, that was not the case. He had another intestinal blockage that was rapidly getting worse. Trying to avoid surgery, they were able once again to thread a tube through his digestive system and relieve the blockage. He finally improved enough to return home after spending an entire month in the hospital.

Gradually, Jonathan improved enough to return to school, and each day provided a new adventure. On days that the weather permitted, Kathy took her little class outside for recess to bask in the sun. Jonathan loved playing on the jungle gym and running to his heart's content.

One particular day when she rounded up her class to go back indoors, she realized Jonathan had vanished from sight. Frantically, she searched the enclosed playground, but he had somehow completely disappeared. Her teacher's aide took the rest of her class indoors as she ran from classroom to classroom asking if anyone had seen him. She could hardly believe where she found him. Apparently, when the "regular" first-grade class had lined up on the playground to go inside, he had positioned himself in line with them and followed them right into their classroom. There he quietly sat at a desk on the back row just as though he belonged there. Since he had no outward appearances that identified him as "handicapped," the teacher had not even noticed him sitting there. Kathy apologized to the teacher and whisked him across the hall to his own class.

Regardless of how hard she tried to discourage it though, Jonathan seemed emotionally drawn to the regular first grade class. It was as though deep down in some hidden area of his being, he knew that he really belonged in that class. At least once a week he wandered off to the regular first grade class. Kathy and the first grade teacher finally decided that as long as he did not disrupt the class, they would allow him to stay for a while. Perhaps something said in the class would even jog his memory of being in first grade and help him to relearn.

Jonathan - Age 4

Age 5 - Easter Sunday

One of many hospital visits   Clown day at the hospital

Favorite Nurse - Marsha

Favorite Nurse - Lisel

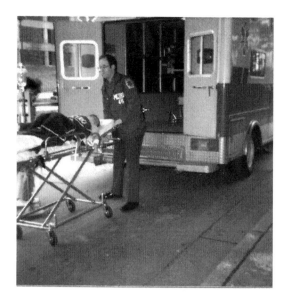

Jonathan's wild
ambulance ride

Jonathan after
taking cortisone
medicine for
many months

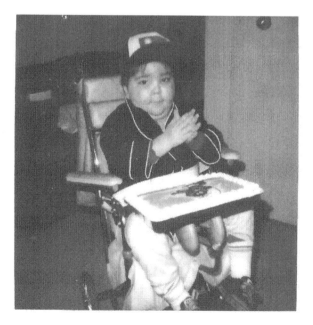

First airplane flight. Going to see grandparents for Christmas

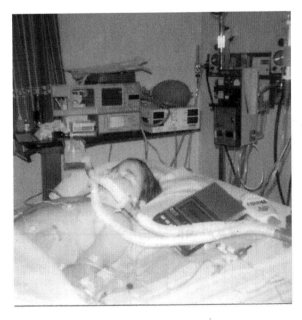

Seventh Birthday Jonathan in coma for two weeks

Jonathan's neighborhood friends gave him a rousing welcome home

At home using sterile procedure to change
Jonathan's bandages

Learning to play ball again

Jonathan as an elf at the Rose
Garden Christmas play

The behavioral psychologist's
prescription for us

Trip to Disney World with Rose
Garden students

SPECIAL OLYMPICS EVENTS

Jamie "catching" Jonathan
at end of race

Second Place ribbon in
Track and Field

Gaining equestrian skills

Jonathan loves to bowl

Our Special Olympics Swimming Champ

Jonathan and Mike enjoying Mike's Harley

HIGH SCHOOL GRADUATION

Jamie gets a kiss from the graduate

'SPECIAL GIFTS' SUNDAY SCHOOL CLASS

Jonathan, Linda Baker, Allyson, Flint, Jill Baker

OUR FAMILY

Kevin   Jamie   Johnny   Jonathan
Will   Sydney   Louise

Chapter 20

Fast-Food Fiasco

Jonathan's hostility continued to be a problem. One afternoon, at the end of Jonathan's school day, Kathy and I were standing in the hall chatting about his progress. Holding his hand and keeping one eye peeled on him as we talked, I noticed the school principal rounding the corner, smiling as he headed our way. I prodded Jonathan as he approached, "Jonathan, say, 'hello' to the principal." He suddenly stiffened, glared at the principal, and screamed in a loud angry tone, "You're dumb and stupid and I hate you!" Completely mortified, speech evaded me. The principal had been so kind and so understanding of our situation. Fortunately, he simply smiled and patted my shoulder as if to say, "I'm sure glad he's yours."

As humiliating as that was, it didn't hold a candle to another problem that had developed. Every day when Jonathan and I left the elementary school headed for his therapy, we pulled into a fast-food restaurant and went through the drive-in area to buy him a soda. Lacking a colon caused him to dehydrate quickly and when he became dehydrated, his seizures became more frequent.

I had learned to place him in the back seat of our car and buckle him in the seat, even if just the two of us were in the car. Unfortunately, I learned that the hard way. Every time I allowed him to sit next to me in the front seat, his hands were in constant motion. He methodically pushed all the radio buttons one after the other, turned the air conditioner controls on and off, and forced the locks on the doors up and down. However, as distracting as all that proved to be, it was not the worst offense. With absolutely no warning whatsoever, he would grab my chin with his hand and yank my face toward him, forcing me to look at him. He only wanted my undivided attention, but the first time he pulled that stunt while I drove through a busy intersection, only God, Himself, protected us from a fatal collision.

So, the first time we approached the fast-food restaurant, Jonathan was safely strapped in his seat belt in the back seat, and I confidently drove up to place our order. I lowered my window and smiled at the teenage girl. "We would like two ..." Before I could finish ordering, Jonathan lowered his window, stretched his little body halfway out the opening and yelled his favorite phrase, "You're dumb and stupid, and I hate you!" The poor girl behind the window looked so dumbfounded and shocked she could not utter a word. I ventured a look in her direction and glimpsed a look of sheer terror plastered on her face. I hastened to assure her he was mentally handicapped and didn't have any personal vendetta against her. She practically threw our sodas at us just to send us quickly on our way.

Unfortunately, it became a pattern. Every time I tried to place an order at a fast-food restaurant, Jonathan screamed his obscenities at the employee. For a while, I tried going to a different fast-food location every day so that each employee would only have to experience this verbal assault one time. That wasn't practical, though, because there were only so many fast-food locations on our route, and we quickly went through them all. I decided maybe it would be better to go to the same location every day and explain Jonathan's situation so that only one person would have to endure his verbal abuse. Of course, that wasn't practical either because it seemed as though a different teenager appeared at the window every day. (I was never sure if the employee turnover rate was that high or if they were pulling strangers off the street to wait on us when they saw my car approaching the restaurant.)

Each time we thought, "surely it can't get any worse than this," Jonathan proved us wrong. Jamie was accompanying us to his therapy session one day when school was out for a teacher workday. We were really enjoying the extra time together, chatting about things going on in her life, when she detected something odd. "Mom, have you noticed people are laughing and pointing at us as they pass our car?" We had a station wagon at the time, and Jonathan had developed a habit of unbuckling his seat belt and crawling in the far back cargo area. We kept toys there to distract him from other pursuits, so I usually just let him stay in the back rather than pulling off the expressway and buckling him back in his seat, only to have to repeat the whole process again a few miles down the road.

Jamie turned to check on Jonathan, but he had crawled to the cargo area and she couldn't see him. By that time, everyone who passed us laughed and pointed at our car. "Jamie, you're going to have to crawl over the seat and see what he is doing," I said. We weren't really sure that we wanted to know, but dutifully, she scrambled her way to the back of the car.

"MOM," she shrieked, as only a teenager knows how, "pull over right now!"

"Jamie, what's wrong?" I could feel my stomach knotting.

"He's NAKED!" she screamed. Sure enough, my eight-year-old son had removed every stitch of his clothing and frolicked happy as a lark, completely nude for the entire world to see.

As humorous as some of his escapades were, his negative behavior was far from amusing. In fact, it was fighting with his medical problems for top billing in my prayer journal. I could deal with his yelling out the window at strangers and even his verbal abuse of his principal and teachers. However, every time he yelled that he hated *me*, it pierced my heart worse than a dagger. Each morning I faced a major struggle simply trying to brush his teeth, get him dressed, and get all his medicine down his throat.

One particular morning he kept saying repeatedly, "You're dumb and stupid, and I hate you." Without warning, something snapped inside me. I grabbed him by the shoulders and began to cry hysterically. My emotional state unraveled completely. I slid to the floor in utter defeat. Suffocating from the grief I felt over my loss of Jonathan, I could not stop the flow of tears. My prayer journal that day reflected my scrambled emotions and painted a picture of the depth of despair that I felt:

"Lord, I can't go on like this. I know that You have promised not to give us more than we can bear, but I can't take this anymore. I have trusted You completely with his health, and You have brought him through countless near-death situations. But, Lord, I am his mother, and I love him so desperately. I can't bear his hatred. I'm so tired and emotionally drained, and You seem so silent. Today is October 26, 1983, and this day I release Jonathan completely to You. Whether You choose to heal him or not to heal him, or even if You choose to take him home to heaven, I accept Your will completely. If You choose to leave him here, I beg You to heal his hostile attitude. I can't endure it much longer. I feel that emotionally I'm hanging by a very thin thread, but I know beyond any doubt that that thread is You."

Oftentimes, God requires that we come to the end of ourselves and totally surrender everything to Him before He can show Himself strong on our behalf.

God began to perform yet another miracle that day. Jonathan didn't change overnight, but God set in motion a complete metamorphosis that day. Over a period of several years, he progressed from yelling, "you're dumb and stupid, and I hate you," to "you're pretty and nice, and I love you." Though this confused the fast-food employees as much as the negative comments had, the employees certainly received it in a more positive light.

He also picked up another comical phrase. Often when we drove up to the fast-food window he leaned out the window and startled the employee by saying to her, "And what would you like to have?" Stealing her line always left her speechless, but at least it produced a smile.

Chapter 21

Thanksgiving Emergency

Jonathan appeared to be doing well physically, so we decided to attempt a trip to visit Johnny's parents for Thanksgiving. He sat quietly during the six-hour drive, but otherwise seemed okay. The minute we walked in the door, the tantalizing aromas of turkey and dressing, sweet potato soufflé, corn casserole, and homemade pecan pie flooded our nostrils. Johnny's mother excelled in the culinary department, and she had prepared a huge Thanksgiving feast with all our favorite recipes. Hungry from the long trip, and certainly not desiring to offend the cook, we did the meal full justice.

Jonathan, as expected, refused to eat anything. He remained quiet and subdued, and I assumed exhaustion from the long journey had set in. We had not attempted a major car trip since he had become handicapped, and I expected him to need extra rest.

I helped clean the kitchen then sat down with the rest of the family to watch television. Around 9:00 p.m., Jonathan crawled up in my lap, and I instantly became alarmed. His forehead burned with fever. We took his temperature and the thermometer registered 104 degrees. In our haste to pack up IV supplies, ostomy supplies, diapers, and seizure medications, I had failed to bring children's fever medication. Johnny and Jamie hurriedly left for the only pharmacy in the area open on Thanksgiving Day.

They had no sooner left than Jonathan began to experience a seizure. It started with a mild focal seizure and quickly escalated to a grand mal seizure. In the midst of the seizure, he began to vomit and gasp for breath. I screamed for Johnny's mom to call the emergency room and let them know we were on our way. Johnny's parents lived about ten miles out of town on a rural country road. I feared an ambulance would take forever to find their house.

We had witnessed many seizures since he had become handicapped, but none as terrifying as this one. Because he continued to vomit, aspiration and choking became real possibilities. He jerked violently and gasped for breath. The seizure seemed to last forever. The thought went through my mind that "this is it; this is the way it will end." After all our struggles to bring him back to health and keep him alive, we're going to lose him, and Johnny is not even here with me. I silently prayed:

"Lord, I feel so totally helpless. You know that one month ago, on October 26, I surrendered Jonathan completely to You. If You have chosen this time to take him home to You, I submit to Your will. But, Lord, if You still have a purpose for him here on earth, please intervene in this crisis and bring him out of this seizure."

The emergency room doctor had instructed us to bring Jonathan to the hospital immediately. We were on our way out the door when his seizure suddenly stopped as abruptly as it had begun, and he fell into a deep sleep. Johnny and Jamie returned, and we bundled him up and set out for the hospital.

The practically deserted streets allowed for faster travel, but the trip into town still seemed endless. A doctor and nurse met us as soon as we pulled up to the emergency room entrance of the small hospital. Since Jonathan's seizure had ended and he had fallen asleep, they seemed very nonchalant about his condition. We tried to explain how critically ill he had been for the past two years, but I could see their lack of interest. The doctor examined him and said the inside of his ear appeared somewhat red. He gave us a prescription for an antibiotic and proceeded to send us on our way. Frantic over the severity of his seizure, I begged the doctor to check the level of seizure medication in his system. I knew it had to be low.

Johnny decided to try to get a call through to Jonathan's doctor in Atlanta. Even though it was late in the evening and Thanksgiving Day, his doctor quickly returned our call, requesting the emergency room doctor to culture his central-line catheter and check his seizure medication levels. I honestly don't think that small hospital had ever seen a patient like Jonathan. The nurse refused to touch his central-line catheter. In a moment of desperation, we told them we knew how to pull the blood through his catheter for the cultures. The nurse seemed amazed but nonetheless relieved. "That's fine with me. What do you need?"

"Nothing except sterile gloves and culture bottles," I replied. "I brought everything else with me." I proceeded to hold up my bag of supplies. She turned to another nurse and said, "Can you believe this?" We would probably be the main topic of conversation at that little hospital for years to come. As I slowly pulled the blood through Jonathan's catheter, the thought of how badly I had wanted to be a nurse years before flashed through my mind. God did indeed work in mysterious ways.

They quickly sent the blood specimens to their lab, gave Jonathan a small dose of Phenobarbitol, and sent us on our way. We returned to my in-laws home very late. We quickly connected his IV equipment to begin his nightly feeding and got ready for bed.

I decided to sleep with Jonathan just to make sure he would be okay. We had not been asleep five minutes when I heard a strange noise coming from his mouth. I turned on the lamp next to the bed and screamed for Johnny to come quickly. Jonathan had vomited again and was going into another grand mal seizure. We dressed hurriedly, grabbed his IV equipment, and headed back to the hospital. Once again, he gasped for breath. Johnny, not having witnessed the previous seizure, wore a look of terror. Jamie and Johnny's mother had insisted on coming with us in the car. Jamie, bundled up in her pajamas and robe and slippers, sat in the back seat huddled next to her grandmother with a look of anxiety written all over her face. She cried softly, then, calmly said, "Dad, I need to tell you something."

"What is it, honey?"

"I just wanted you to know that I've had CPR training at school, and I know how to do it if you need me to." We should have known at that instant that she was destined to be a doctor one day.

Once again, by the time we arrived at the emergency room, the seizure had ended, and Jonathan had fallen into a deep sleep. Under different circumstances, the facial expressions of the hospital personnel when we returned to the emergency room would have been a source of great humor. Johnny had Jonathan in his arms, and I followed close behind transporting his IV pump and the feeding bottles, holding the plastic tubing that connected Jonathan to the machine high in the air.

This time a different doctor arrived who seemed more capable of handling the situation. Jonathan's fever had dropped to 101, but this doctor didn't think his ears were inflamed enough to cause the fever. "I can't decide if it would be best to admit him to the hospital or to keep him in the emergency room until morning for observation. Do you have a preference?" We appreciated her seeking our input.

Since the clock registered 3:00 a.m., and we desperately wanted to return to his doctor in Atlanta as soon as possible, we chose to stay in the emergency room. Realizing how exhausted we all were, they pushed Jonathan's gurney into a room with two other gurneys so Johnny and I could attempt to get some sleep. Johnny's mother took Jamie home with her, and Johnny and I settled in for the remainder of the night.

The nurse checked on Jonathan frequently. Thankfully, he seemed to have stabilized. We learned from the lab report the next morning that his seizure medications had been dangerously low for some unknown reason and had caused the two grand mal seizures.

Jonathan slept peacefully the rest of the night, and the following morning we put in another call to his doctor in Atlanta. He instructed us to meet him at Scottish Rite as soon as we returned to Atlanta. Fortunately, Jonathan slept most of the way home. They performed numerous tests but never determined exactly what had caused such a high fever.

Following this harrowing experience, Jonathan's doctor strongly recommended that Johnny and I both receive training in CPR. We promptly located a Red Cross class near our home, completed the course, and obtained our certificates. At least, another emergency would find all three of us trained and prepared.

Chapter 22

Addressing the Problems

We continued to experience mounting frustration because of Jonathan's ongoing medical and behavioral problems. Towards the end of 1983, we approached his doctors about the possibility of a comprehensive, overall evaluation. His gastrointestinal doctor offered to contact the pediatric neurological staff at the Medical College of Georgia (MCG) in Augusta. He asked them to consider evaluating Jonathan's worsening seizure disorder, his poor appetite, which necessitated IV feeding therapy at home, and his severe language and behavioral deficits. Since MCG is a teaching hospital, they welcomed the challenge that Jonathan presented.

We scheduled his initial evaluation for January 18, 1984, which allowed us to spend the last few days of 1983 with my family celebrating the birth of our Savior and focusing our attention on happier events.

On January 18 we arrived on schedule and signed in at the front desk. A nurse directed us to the pediatric neurology clinic. We spent the following hour filling out reams of paperwork documenting his extensive medical history from birth to the present. Finally, a team of doctors, dressed in their starched whites, came in to meet Jonathan. We were impressed with their kindness, thoroughness, and sensitivity to our situation. Johnny and I spent the rest of that day answering questions while the doctors secured blood samples and Jonathan underwent x-rays. Completely drained—physically and emotionally—we headed back to Atlanta.

The neurology team promised to contact us soon after documenting their evaluation and recommendations.

The following letter (in part) arrived on February 1:

Dear Mr. and Mrs. Flanders:

I am addressing this letter to you because you will have to make the decision for Jonathan about what role we might play in his care. You must have sensed the feelings of all of us during your visit; fascinated and overwhelmed by problems yet respecting and admiring your family and your physicians for how you have handled what few of us feel confident in our own ability to handle either personally or professionally.

I did have an opportunity to talk with your pediatrician who was with Jonathan at the onset of his post-operative complication last year. From his description, I would feel the insult probably was a   stroke. The non-contrasted CT scan, which was the only safe neurological procedure to perform at that time, does not usually show the effects of interruption of blood supply, only demonstrating hemorrhages into the brain. The other reason I think this is that Jonathan has had two large vessel thromboses (blood clots) complicating his hyperalimentation (IV feeding). His seizures which now are usually triggered by the hyperalimentation, appear to arise in the left hemisphere, and he does show a rather striking receptive aphasia, (the loss or impairment of the power to use or comprehend words as a result of brain damage) again pointing to some damage to the left hemisphere. I do not think the mechanism of the brain injury is that important to know in our plans for Jonathan's future, but you had asked me and I wanted to express my best guess.

With a lot of help from my colleagues, I can offer you the following:

1) Attempting to address Jonathan's apparent loss of normal appetite.

2) Documenting with serial blood studies, what happens to his metabolism of foodstuffs and drugs during IV feeding that triggers the seizures.

3) And attempting to change Jonathan's seizure medication to a drug that could be modified if necessary on days he receives IV feedings.

There are many other challenges in his management which I feel your physicians and the other professionals in Atlanta would be in a much better position to deal with including his continuing rehabilitation, the exploration of alternate methods of feeding him, and continuing support for your family unit, both emotionally and financially.

In order to accomplish the goals I outlined above, I believe it would probably be necessary to have Jonathan here in the hospital for a two week period.

I would like for you to think about this, talk to your doctors, and let me know if you would like for me to make the arrangements. I would like very much to have Jonathan come back, but I will respect whatever decision you make.

We discussed the letter with Jonathan's doctors, and everyone agreed that we needed to explore every option available for his total recovery. We contacted the doctors in Augusta to make the necessary arrangements for Jonathan to come. Johnny had planned to drive Jonathan and me to Augusta, stay until we settled in, and then return to Atlanta to work and to be home for Jamie. Jonathan and I would stay at the hospital as long as necessary. We scheduled March 19 as his admission date. I dreaded being so far from home, where we knew no one, but we were excited about the possibility of unraveling some of the medical mysteries that surrounded Jonathan.

Often it seemed as if time were standing still where Jonathan was concerned. I recorded the following statement in my prayer journal:

Lengthy afflictions need not discourage us. Joseph's afflictions began at age 17 and continued until he was 30. The Bible does not record even a hint of discouragement during his 13 years of trials.

I couldn't honestly say we had not experienced discouragement along the way, but we were definitely committed for the long haul. Our three years of struggling with Jonathan's medical crises paled in comparison to Joseph's thirteen years of afflictions, involving slavery, false accusations by Potiphar's wife, and imprisonment for many years. In spite of all the terrible circumstances Joseph endured, one frequently repeated phrase in Genesis 39 stuck like glue in my mind: "the Lord was with Joseph." It's easy to assume when life's problems seem overwhelming that God has forgotten us. Genesis 39 assures us that that is not the case. God used the circumstances in Joseph's life to mature him and to prepare him for what lay ahead. Joseph endured, and we would, too, with God's help.

Chapter 23

A Week of Testing

March 19 rolled around quickly, and we were on our way back to Augusta. It didn't take long to check in, get our room assignment, and unpack. I tried to be as positive as possible when Johnny and Jamie left, but truthfully, fear overruled every other emotion.

The first night after the nurse had begun Jonathan's IV therapy and he had drifted off to sleep, I struggled to recall a verse that God had given me the previous week. Overcome with anxiety before we left for Augusta, my stomach had been in knots, and doubts had stolen my peace and constantly bombarded my mind.

What if Jonathan never gets any better; or what if he regresses? Or what if he dies? What if the doctors in Augusta find something else wrong with him that no one even knew about? What if they find out his brain damage is so severe he can never progress any further? What if ... What if ... what if ...

On and on the assaults came. I had learned by then to fight those doubts and fears with the only weapons that were effective: prayer and God's Word. God had begun to develop in me a strong love for His Word and particularly a desire to read from the book of Psalms daily. That particular day, I opened my Bible to Psalm 112 and began to read. When I got to verses seven and eight, the words jumped off the page and spoke directly to my heart. The Living Bible (TLB) says, "He does not fear bad news, nor live in dread of what may happen. For he is settled in his mind that Jehovah will take care of him. That is why he is not afraid."

I accepted the fact that that verse *did not* say that nothing bad would ever happen to us, and I received great comfort from the fact that it *did* say that we did not need to worry about our future. God has promised to take care of us.

The Lord also brought to my mind another story that illustrated God's faithfulness. II Kings 19 reveals that King Hezekiah received a letter from the king of Assyria threatening to overtake and destroy Jerusalem in the same way that Assyria had destroyed many other nations. Look closely at Hezekiah's response. Hezekiah read the letter, and rather than giving up in despair, he immediately went to the house of the Lord, spread the letter before the Lord, and prayed for God to deliver them. God answered his prayer by miraculously destroying the Assyrian army encamped around Jerusalem. God used Hezekiah's faith to strengthen my own faith. Even though he must have been very afraid, Hezekiah's first instinct was to lay his burden before God and pray.

I had Jonathan's previous CAT scan films with me since the doctors at MCG wanted to study them. That night I slid the films from their folder and spread them across my cot, just as Hezekiah had spread his letter before God. I knelt by my bed and once again surrendered Jonathan's outcome and future to God. I asked God to take away my fear and to help me to remember that no matter what happened to Jonathan, God remained in control, and He would take care of all of us.

The following week consisted of a parade of doctors, nurses, residents, and medical students questioning, prodding, probing, and testing Jonathan. He required monitoring 24 hours a day, and I quickly became "stir-crazy." Getting to the cafeteria for meals, taking showers—everything presented a challenge. With each passing day, I felt myself becoming more and more depressed. We had had a wonderful support system in Atlanta with friends calling and visiting constantly. In Augusta, the phone had been silent and visits non-existent.

The crowning blow came on Thursday. The neurologists wanted a psychiatrist to evaluate Jonathan. With our one and only experience with a psychiatrist still fresh in my memory bank, I was understandably reluctant. However, we had come to MCG for a thorough evaluation, and the psychiatrist just might have some insight into his continued hyperactivity and his lack of appetite.

Our appointment with the psychiatrist began with the usual questions about Jonathan's history. By this time, I had been required to recite it so many times I was considering recording it on a cassette tape and handing a copy to each doctor. While I answered the doctor's questions, Jonathan began twirling around and around with his head thrown back gazing up at the light fixture.

"Does he do that often?" the psychiatrist questioned.

"Not often, but occasionally," I replied. "Why do you ask?"

"He is demonstrating some unusual symptoms. Would you mind if I videotaped him?" he asked. "The tape would be confidential, of course, and used for teaching purposes only."

I had no idea what to say. I desperately wanted to talk it over with Johnny before saying "yes," but of course, that was not possible. The doctor had his equipment set up and began moving us towards his studio. "I suppose that will be okay," I agreed reluctantly.

He started the camera rolling, and I immediately regretted having consented. Jonathan began exhibiting some bizarre behaviors that were abnormal even for him, with the video camera recording it for all eternity. I felt like I had betrayed Jonathan somehow, and my stomach recoiled in response. I yearned to grab Jonathan and flee from the room. I murmured something about needing to get Jonathan back to his room for his medications and raced out the door as quickly as I could with Jonathan in tow.

Back in the safety of our room, my fragile emotional state began to unravel. Worn to a frazzle, a whopper-sized migraine headache began to work its way from the back of my head to the front. The constant stress of the week had left me totally depleted.

Johnny had planned to come on Saturday to stay for the weekend, but I didn't think I could stand the pressure another day. I called him that evening and begged him to take a day of vacation and come the next day. Sensing correctly that one finger could easily push me over the edge; he readily agreed to come early.

The next morning when he arrived, I brought him up-to-date on Jonathan's tests and the unsettling psychiatric appointment. Encircling me in his arms, he reassured me that the hospital would keep Jonathan's tape confidential and I did not need to worry.

Johnny quickly realized that I desperately needed a break. He made a reservation at a motel across the street that offered discounts to patients' family members, and he stayed in the room with Jonathan. We had made plans for Jamie to spend the weekend with a friend, and Johnny didn't have to return to Atlanta until Sunday.

Johnny and I had dinner together in Jonathan's room, and then I made a hasty retreat to the motel. I took a long shower and curled up in bed with a book. I slowly felt the tensions of the previous week melt away. My eyes closed in sleep long before I finished one page.

The next morning when I returned to the hospital, a wonderful surprise awaited me. The doctors had managed to complete all their tests in one week instead of two. We could return to Atlanta that afternoon. I could not have been happier. We packed up everything in Jonathan's room in record time and headed home.

Jonathan rested on the trip back home, and Johnny caught me up on the local news. We pulled into our driveway and were surprised to see a car parked in front of our house. Roger Hines, a close friend of ours from our church, knelt in our flowerbeds busily pulling weeds. He had already mowed and edged our grass and began apologizing profusely for not having finished before we arrived home. Another friend had obtained a key to our house from our neighbor and had cleaned it from top to bottom.

As a result of our trip to Augusta, Jonathan's neurologist made several changes to Jonathan's medication that resulted in better seizure control. We also learned that his lack of appetite did not result from neurological damage. The area of the brain responsible for creating appetite appeared to be functioning normally. Even though they were not able to detect the exact cause of his lack of appetite, we were encouraged by this information because it meant that, with time, possibly his normal desire to eat would return.

The doctors confirmed that Jonathan's brain damage appeared to be permanent. The scans revealed a considerable amount of atrophy resulting in diffuse (scattered) brain damage. Though hard to accept, that news did not come as a surprise. God had mercifully given us a year to adjust to the fact that the "Jonathan" that we had previously known would never exist again. God had given us time to grow spiritually and mature in our faith. He had given us time to learn to trust Him regardless of our circumstances.

Chapter 24

A Stinkin' Greasy Baptism

With all the trips back and forth to the hospital, speech and behavior therapy, and school almost daily for three years, the car that I drove every day was on its last leg. I've often joked that Johnny insists that we drive our cars until they are begging and pleading, "please release me and let me go in peace to junk-yard heaven!" My current car was crying for mercy. However, the cost of the necessary repairs far exceeded our stretched budget. Once again, we turned to the Bible for answers.

Philippians 4:6 states, "Be anxious for nothing, but in everything by prayer and supplication, with thanksgiving, let your requests be made known to God." Philippians 4:19 promises, "My God shall supply all your need according to His riches in glory by Christ Jesus." Psalm 34:10b declares, "Those who seek the Lord shall not lack any good thing."

We prayed about our need for a car and waited for God's response. Not long after we began to pray, we had a phone call from my dad. "Your mom and I have been concerned about the excessive number of miles your car has on it and the repairs that it needs. Here's what we want you to do. Purchase whatever you need to transport Jonathan safely, and we will make the payments as long as you need for us to. We have been praying for the Lord to show us some way we could help you, and this is something we would like to do."

We had not shared our need of a car with anyone, including my parents, so we felt that their offer was definitely God's answer to our prayer. Nevertheless, it was very difficult for Johnny to accept my parents' offer. He had always taken great pride in being able to provide for his family. Even during the years that I had worked outside the home, I had always known that anytime I wanted to quit it would have been okay with him. However, we had accumulated so many medical bills over the past three years that we had no surplus for a down payment or a monthly payment on a car.

My dad was very persuasive, however, and Johnny finally agreed, with the understanding that as soon as we were able, we would take over the payments and reimburse my parents. The next Saturday we seriously began car hunting. About mid-afternoon, we were walking up and down rows and rows of cars for sale, preoccupied with eager salesmen and searching for a bargain.

Jonathan ran carefree between the rows of cars, expending pent-up energy since he was feeling exceptionally good that day. Johnny and I attempted to keep one eye peeled on him. It hit me suddenly that it had grown quiet—too quiet. I couldn't see Jonathan anywhere. Johnny and I frantically began to race between the cars calling his name. Where could he have gone? We had seen him just moments before. Sheer panic had begun to set in when we heard a loud cry for help.

Heading in the direction of Jonathan's voice, we were completely unprepared for what we saw. Apparently, some workers had left the cover off a grease pit, and Jonathan had fallen into the hole. Even though the grease pit appeared to be on the property of the car lot, it actually belonged to a seafood restaurant next door. We found Jonathan neck-deep in—you guessed it—stale fish grease! We carefully hauled him out of the pit, concerned that he could have broken bones or sprained muscles. We did a quick assessment, and he appeared to be okay except for one thing: He stank to high heaven! Imagine the odor from the refuse of a seafood restaurant.

We didn't know what to do with him. He smelled so awful we couldn't take him inside the restaurant or the car sales office to wash him off. Neither did we relish putting him in the car we were attempting to trade in. Finally, Johnny decided to go in the sales office to see if they had anything we could use. The best they could offer was some plastic trash bags. We used them to cover the seat of the car and carefully positioned Jonathan on the bags. All the way home he kept repeating, "Mommy, get it off, get it off." The stench was so overpowering we could barely stay in the car with him.

We raced home as quickly as possible. We were primarily concerned about his central-line catheter positioned near his heart. Protruding from the center of his chest and completely covered with a sealed dressing, it nevertheless posed a major health risk. If even a miniscule leak occurred, the waste from the grease pit could seep into his heart through the contaminated catheter.

We finally arrived home where we stripped off all his clothes in the basement and promptly threw them in the trash. Even naked he still smelled like a garbage dump. We led him upstairs and started the shower. While Johnny attempted to clean him, I placed a call to his doctor. "You won't believe what happened to Jonathan today," I began.

"Mrs. Flanders, I would believe anything you told me about Jonathan," he replied. He obviously knew Jonathan well.

I explained our predicament. He instructed us to scrub Jonathan all over, from head to toe, even his hair, with betadine (the brown, sticky stuff they smear all over you for disinfecting prior to surgery). We were to use sterile technique, as we always did, to change his central-line dressing and were to bring him to the doctor's office the next week for lab work.

As soon as we got him cleaned up, Johnny placed a call to the restaurant. They were very non-apologetic until they realized the grease pit was indeed on their property, and they could be libel for any problems that resulted from his fall. Considering all Jonathan's past medical problems, they realized they could be in a lot of trouble for leaving the cover off the pit.

Amazingly enough, follow-up studies revealed no problems whatsoever resulting from his grease pit immersion. Only one problem lingered. Many months passed by before we could even think about eating at a seafood restaurant again.

We encountered another situation at a local restaurant not long after the "grease pit" episode. Jamie had gone on a church outing one Friday night, so the three of us decided to eat at a local barbeque restaurant we had never before visited. There were few empty seats in the restaurant when we arrived, so we assumed the food must be extraordinary. The server seated us quickly, and we enjoyed a wonderful meal. Jonathan behaved nicely, and we congratulated ourselves that we had made it through the entire meal with no embarrassing episodes.

With appetites satiated and everyone in a happy mood, we proceeded to leave the restaurant. We had made it a practice to hold Jonathan's hand whenever possible because of his proclivity for running away and his overall unpredictable behavior. Johnny would hold one hand, and I would firmly grip the other. Unfortunately, the tables were crammed very closely together in that particular restaurant, and we had to maneuver our way out single file. It shouldn't have been a problem. I went first, and Johnny brought up the rear with Jonathan sandwiched between us. We were almost home free, close to the exit door, when I heard Johnny gasp. Recognizing that sound, I knew whatever had transpired could not be good. I turned around reluctantly to see what had happened.

Apparently, as Jonathan passed by one of the tables, he decided, for reasons known only to him, to plop his entire hand right smack down in the middle of a man's plate of food. The man's mouth flew open and a look of indescribable shock registered on his face.

Johnny apologized profusely and tried to explain that because of Jonathan's mental disability he didn't understand what he had done. Johnny offered to buy the man another meal, but the man insisted he had almost finished anyway, and that wouldn't be necessary. I jerked Jonathan out of the restaurant as rapidly as I could and confined him in the car. Johnny paid the bill and joined us a few minutes later. For a while we just sat in the car in stunned silence. Then we thought about how funny the whole episode must have looked to everyone in the restaurant. The more we thought about it, the funnier it became. Doubled over in stitches, with tears running down our faces, we literally couldn't stop laughing.

The Bible says in Proverbs 17:22, "A merry heart does good like medicine ..." We had a good dose of God's medicine that day in spite of Jonathan's wayward behavior.

Chapter 25

Salt of the Earth Friends

We had made it well past the one-year mark since Jonathan's stroke, and we had accepted the fact that, short of a major miracle from God, Jonathan would be permanently mentally handicapped. The time had come for us to think about a plan for his future. We heard about a class offered for parents of special needs children conducted by an attorney who specialized in writing wills for families with disabled family members. We signed up to attend and were very impressed with the lawyer's expertise in that area. We scheduled an appointment with him at his office for the following week.

He discussed areas with us that we probably would not have thought about on our own. The attorney instructed us to take a work sheet home and complete it before the next appointment. The last section of the work sheet had us stumped. We had to include in the will the names of guardians for Jamie and Jonathan in the event that Johnny and I both died at the same time. Even though it was highly unlikely that that would ever happen we could not omit that important part of our will.

We searched through our repertoire of relatives. I had a sister and two brothers, and Johnny had one sister, but none of them lived near us. They were all scattered across several states. We felt that it would be important to Jonathan's health to keep him in familiar surroundings and to continue with the doctors who were aware of his medical history. We prayed about this important decision and racked our brains. Then we prayed about it some more, agonizing over the decision.

We both kept thinking of a couple from our church who had been close friends of ours for many years—Roger and Nancy Hines (the same Roger who had been on his hands and knees weeding our flowerbeds when we had returned from Augusta.) Roger and Nancy were "salt of the earth" people. Both public school teachers, Sunday school teachers, and Roger a fellow deacon with Johnny, they didn't come any better. We had taken turns babysitting each other's children in the past, so they knew our kids well. We loved them like family. Our daughter Jamie and their daughter Christy shared the same birthday, and the two of them were close friends.

We knew that if Roger and Nancy agreed to take care of Jamie and Jonathan, they would love and care for them as they would their own children. Johnny and I strongly sensed God's leadership in asking them to consider accepting this responsibility, in spite of the fact that they already had four children of their own.

We set up a time to take them out for coffee and dessert and told them we needed to talk to them about something very important. We met them at a restaurant and chatted for a while over coffee. I knew they had to be bursting with curiosity about why we had asked them to meet with us. We finally got up our nerve and plunged ahead with our request.

"It's extremely unlikely that you will ever be called upon to fulfill this responsibility, but it's vital that we make provision for our children, especially Jonathan, in the event that something should happen to both of us," Johnny explained. We assured them that when Jamie, already fifteen years old, completed college; she would assume the responsibility of caring for Jonathan, if it became necessary. "Believe me, we know better than anyone exactly what we are asking of your family," we emphasized. The proposal we presented to them involved an awesome, overwhelming commitment.

"Please understand that we will not be offended or upset with you and Nancy in any way—ever—if you feel that you cannot or should not agree to do this," Johnny told them. "Your decision will never change our friendship or our love for you and your family in any way. Please take as long as you need to think about this and pray about it."

We were completely unprepared for their response. Roger didn't hesitate a minute. "I know Nancy well enough that I think I can speak for both of us," Roger began as his eyes filled with tears. "You can't imagine how honored we feel that you would even consider asking us to care for your children if needed. Our answer, of course, is 'yes.'" Nancy nodded her head in agreement. Their quick, positive response completely stunned us.

Years later, we were reminded once again of the precious commitment that Roger and Nancy made to our family. Roger ran for public office and won the election to serve in the Georgia House of Representatives. He and Nancy were busier than ever, but they took the time to pen the following note (in part):

It's been on my mind for over two years, or at least since Jamie's wedding, to write the two of you a note. At Jamie's wedding, the minister mentioned that Jamie had told Kevin, her fiancé, before they married that it would one day be their responsibility to care for Jonathan. I just wanted to say that if anything happens to either or both of you before your biblically allotted days, Jamie and Kevin will not be alone in caring for Jonathan. Even though Jamie is of age, the commitment that Nancy and I made to you years ago was forever.

We were speechless when we received that note. No words could adequately explain the depth of gratitude we felt for their expression of love.

Chapter 26

Facing Goliath

Jonathan continued to vacillate back and forth health-wise. Between 1981 and 1983, he had spent almost a year in the hospital, including several weeks in ICU. A whole year! Not only were *we* concerned about his on-going health problems and the medical bills associated with long-term illness, but our health insurance company had also begun to take notice. In April of 1984 a representative of Jonathan's health insurance company contacted us. They wanted to see first-hand this child who had drained so much of their company's money.

The meeting had my nerves on edge. Several of the representatives from the insurance company planned to attend. What if they decided to stop or limit his coverage? Johnny could not leave work for the meeting, so Jonathan and I had to face Goliath alone.

They began the meeting by asking me to give them a summary of Jonathan's medical history. (I knew I should have made that cassette tape!) I began to relate everything that had happened to him. I pulled up his shirt and exposed his scars from his numerous surgeries. I showed them the central-line catheter required for his daily IV feedings, and the dressing in the center of his chest that had to remain sterile at all times. I introduced them to "Charlie," his ileostomy bag, and I lined up all of his seizure medications and the other medications necessary to keep him alive. By the time I finished, we had to send out for boxes of tissue. They were literally in tears. Even the tough-looking men from the insurance company had tears coursing down their cheeks. I secretly thought maybe I had missed my calling in life, that I really should have been a lawyer. Instead of complaining about how much money Jonathan had cost their company, they began asking what they could do to help make our lives easier.

Since the insurance company appeared to be in a generous mood, I decided to seize the moment. *Carpe diem.* I requested a nurse to come to our home a few hours a month so that Johnny and I could have some desperately needed time away. To our total amazement, they readily agreed.

The next week we contacted a nursing service and scheduled an appointment to have them meet Jonathan and assess his medical needs. As soon as we received approval for services, Johnny and I established a "date night" and instructed the agency to send a nurse to our home. I eagerly awaited our first evening out together, but I also felt somewhat nervous about leaving Jonathan with a stranger. Jamie had plans for the evening and wouldn't be home until late, so I couldn't count on her to give us a blow-by-blow account of the evening. We had never before left Jonathan with a stranger, but after all, the sitter would be a nurse trained to handle any situation. Right?

The doorbell rang right on time. Expecting a female nurse, I found myself face to face with a thin middle-aged man. I'm sure shock registered on my face. (Even though there are now plenty of male nurses, they were somewhat rare in 1984.) Shabbily dressed and somewhat unkempt in appearance, he marched right past me into the den and began asking questions about Jonathan. Knots began to form in my stomach. Before I knew it, he had ushered Johnny and me out the door and closed it firmly behind us. Johnny's suspicions ran high, and he ran to the driveway to write down the man's license plate number. From the looks of things, it appeared that the man's car housed his entire wardrobe and all of his earthly belongings. By that time, my apprehension level scored above twenty on a scale of one to ten. I could hardly bring myself to get in our car. We drove a couple of blocks in silence. By the third block, we blurted out simultaneously, "Let's go home!"

We quickly turned around and raced back home. We told the man that we weren't emotionally ready to leave Jonathan yet, but we would sign his papers to ensure his payment for the evening. He smiled, apparently thrilled with payment for doing no work, and we had a renewed excitement about spending the evening with Jonathan and forfeiting our date.

The next month brought two unexpected blessings. Jonathan began to ride the bus to school for the first time since his stroke. He continued to have a short school day extending from 10:00 to 2:30. In order to accommodate his schedule, a special education bus came to our house about 9:30 just for him. He literally had the bus to himself. He also rode the bus home from school the one day of the week that I didn't have to take him to therapy. For the first time since he had become sick, I had a small amount of free time. It had been so long since I had had any "me" time, I had no idea what to do with myself. I had spent practically every minute of my life the previous two-and-a-half years taking care of Jonathan. I quickly adapted to the welcome transition.

The second blessing came as a total surprise. People frequently asked us why we had never filed a lawsuit on Jonathan's behalf. I even overheard someone say upon hearing Jonathan's history, "Wow, the Flanders must be millionaires by now from lawsuits." We had chosen not to sue anyone for one simple reason: We knew that everything Jonathan's doctors had done had been for one purpose only—to restore him completely back to health. Everything they had done had been in his best interest, and we had complete confidence in them. It is important to remember that Jonathan had had an extremely complicated and unusual medical condition. None of his doctors had ever seen a case of ulcerative colitis so severe in a five-year-old child. I do believe that accountability is essential if a doctor or hospital is negligent or careless, however, we did not feel that applied to our situation. We also knew that even if we successfully sued and won thousands of dollars, it would not restore Jonathan's damaged brain or give back to us the child that we had lost. We did struggle financially, but we knew that if we honored Christ in the decisions we made, He would supply all our needs, just as He promised.

The Bible reveals in Matthew 6:31, 32b, 33, "Therefore do not worry, saying, 'What shall we eat?' or 'What shall we drink?' or 'What shall we wear?' ...For your heavenly Father knows that you need all these things. But seek first the kingdom of God and His righteousness, and all these things shall be added to you." Psalm 50:10, 12b, and 15 declare, "For every beast of the forest is Mine, and the cattle on a thousand hills. For the world is Mine and all its fullness. Call upon Me in the day of trouble; I will deliver you, and you shall glorify Me."

We simply trusted the God of the universe who owns everything to take care of us. And He did, in a unique and awesome way.

One day after retrieving the mail from the mailbox, I casually flipped through the bills and sales ads. My eyes spotted an unusual envelope. It included our name and address on the front. It was neatly typed, but the envelope strangely omitted a return address. It did contain an Atlanta postmark. I assumed we had received a note of encouragement or a card from a friend. The contents almost sent me into shock.

The short, typewritten note stated that though we had never mentioned it to anyone, our financial situation had to be tight, considering Jonathan's extended illness. The person sending the letter wanted to help. The letter was signed (typed) simply: "a Christian friend." Enclosed along with the letter was a cashier's check for $5,000. The "purchased by" area of the check was blank. Over the following year, we received an anonymous check every two or three months, each for $2,000 or $3,000. The checks' arrival dates always coincided with the arrival of bills from the hospital or doctors, even though our mystery donor had no way of knowing when we received those bills. It reminded me of I Timothy 6:18: "Let them do good, that they be rich in good works, ready to give, willing to share,"

The Lord not only used that generous person to help us financially, but because our benefactor remained anonymous, we never felt the burden of trying to repay, and we never suffered any embarrassment because of the lavish gifts. We never knew who sent the checks, but we always knew Whom to thank. I still to this day often ask God to bless the anonymous friend who God used to bless us.

"But when you do a charitable deed, do not let your left hand know what your right hand is doing, that your charitable deed may be in secret; and your Father who sees in secret will Himself reward you openly." (Matthew 6:3-4).

Chapter 27

Beach Catastrophe

Jonathan spent another week hospitalized in May of 1984. Physically and emotionally exhausted, I looked forward to summer with school out and a chance to get some much-needed rest.

Jonathan gradually improved and appeared stronger each day. About halfway through the summer, Johnny suggested that Jamie and I take an extended weekend and go to Florida for some rest and relaxation. He said he would take a few days of vacation and care of Jonathan. It sounded too good to be true. When Jonathan had been so critically ill following his stroke, I had dreamed of escaping to the beach and basking in the sun.

Jamie would be starting her sophomore year in the fall, and I realized that all too soon she would graduate and be off to college. A trip together would allow me to give her my undivided attention, at least for a few days—something she rarely got at home. It would also give me a break from the constant care that Jonathan required. I had been with him night and day for so long that a few days soaking up the sun and doing nothing but resting and reading sounded like a dream come true. Johnny didn't have to ask twice. Jamie and I packed our bags and arranged to stay at a hotel right on the beach.

Jamie had recently obtained her driving learner's permit that allowed her to drive with a licensed adult in the car. She had taken driver's education and spent many hours practicing with Johnny, who proved to have much more patience than I did. She had always driven responsibly, so I promised her that she could drive part of the trip, but only on the open road away from large cities. We laughed about that promise for years after our trip!

We set out bright and early and had a fun, uneventful trip to Florida. I called Johnny as soon as we checked into our hotel to let him know we had arrived safely. "Have a great time and don't worry about Jonathan and me," he told us.

We felt like birds out of a cage. We slipped off our shoes and took a long walk on the beach, enjoying the rushing sound of the waves, the back and forth chirping of the sand pipers, and the feel of the warm, coarse sand squishing between our toes. After enjoying a delicious seafood dinner, we turned in early and slept soundly.

The next morning we wolfed down bowls of cereal in our room and prepared to head to the beach. We had stocked the refrigerator in our room with breakfast and lunch foods, allowing us to spend all day on the beach. We hurried outside where a gorgeous, Florida sun welcomed us to the beach. We immediately rented two beach lounge chairs with a huge umbrella between them. Leaving our beach towels, books, magazines, sunscreen lotion, and cassette player and tapes on our chairs, we trudged through the sand towards the water.

We spent all morning frolicking in the waves, napping on the beach, reading books and magazines, listening to music, and talking—lots of talking. Just what I needed. We went back to our room around noon and stayed just long enough to gobble down some sandwiches and cookies before heading back outside.

About mid-afternoon, we decided to go for a walk down the beach to a refreshment stand to get some cold sodas. Jamie wasn't wearing her glasses or contact lenses, so I decided to wear my glasses to ensure that one of us could see. (I am extremely near-sighted with astigmatism, which means I can barely see my hand in front of my face without my glasses.)

About halfway to the refreshment stand, we began to perspire. The scorching Florida sun seemed relentless. "Why don't we wade out in the water just far enough to dip down and get wet and cool off," I suggested.

It sounded like a great idea. I had no idea a catastrophe lurked ahead. About the time I squatted down with only my head above water, a huge wave came rolling in and completely engulfed my whole body, knocking me sideways. The wave retreated as quickly as it had come in, but as I stood up, I immediately realized a disaster had occurred. My glasses were missing! I frantically called for Jamie to help me look for them. We both spent the next few hours combing the entire area, to no avail. Apparently, they had washed out to sea with the wave.

I felt sick to my stomach. What were we going to do? I couldn't believe I had been so careless. "Don't worry, Mom," Jamie said trying to console me. "You can wear my glasses, and I'll wear my contacts." I thought it might work, and I certainly didn't have a better solution. We both suffered from near-sightedness, but I had a much stronger prescription. We spent the rest of the afternoon on the beach, but my inability to see definitely put a damper on our trip. We checked with the hotel management several times to see if anyone had spotted my glasses washed up on the beach, but that proved hopeless.

That evening Jamie wanted to go to a movie, so I decided to try her glasses. Her watered-down prescription helped somewhat, but I still could not see well. I managed to drive the short distance to the theater, but the movie presented a different problem. My head began to throb from wearing incorrect lenses. Not wanting to do anything to spoil Jamie's vacation, I pretended that I could see okay, but about halfway through the movie, I removed her glasses and sat there blindly staring at the fuzzy screen.

We spent the next day on the beach and then packed to return home. Suddenly, reality set in. How in the world were we going to get home? I frantically called Johnny. "I don't think I can see well enough with Jamie's glasses to drive safely, plus I developed a splitting headache after wearing them less than an hour. It's a seven-hour drive to Atlanta. What are we going to do?" My voice inched an octave higher, a few decibels louder, and became more panic-stricken with each word.

Johnny very calmly replied, "Let Jamie drive home. I've spent a lot of time teaching her, and I know she's a good driver. Thankfully, she has her learner's permit so there shouldn't be a problem."

"Are you nuts?" I said. Too much sun and groping around blindly for two days had taken a toll on me.

"It will be a good experience for her," he countered. Easy for him to say. He didn't have to be the passenger. It finally sank in that we didn't have another option. Jamie jumped up and down with joy.

"Don't worry, Mom. I'll get us home safely," she assured me. Oh, the cockiness of youth. However, she did exactly that. We stopped for gas about an hour outside of Atlanta, and I called Johnny to let him know where we were and to remind him to pray for our safety driving through Atlanta. She maneuvered from I-85 to I-285, the huge perimeter interstate around Atlanta, then from I-285 onto I-75 without a mishap. The experience did a lot for her confidence and a lot for my prayer life.

Chapter 28

Call the Right Doctor

F all rolled around quickly, and soon Jamie and Jonathan were both back in school. We quickly settled into a routine. Jonathan, almost nine years old, had improved in some areas, but still struggled overall. We received a report prepared by the school psychologist dated October 1984. Though painful to read, it represented an accurate assessment of Jonathan's functioning level. The report included the following observations:

Jonathan was seen for one evaluative session at his school. He was observed on two occasions at his school. Jonathan was observed as he put some puzzles together and solved some simple matching tasks. He was also observed interacting with his teacher. Throughout the session, it was difficult to determine whether Jonathan's failures were due to an inability to perform the task or unwillingness to do so. His behavior throughout appeared to be characterized by non-compliance and opposition to requests.

Jonathan was also observed as he went to lunch with his class. Jonathan walked or sat near the teacher at all times. Since he brings his lunch from home, he was guided to the cooler, where he was able to get his milk for lunch. He sat down at the table and began to eat. He remained relatively quiet in one place for approximately ten minutes. During this time, he pulled his sandwich into bites and stuck the pieces on the ends of his fingers. He then ate the pieces off the end of each finger. At one point, he leaned over the table and picked the food up with his mouth. After the initial ten minutes, Jonathan took his shoe and sock off and put his sock and foot on the table. The teacher got up and made him put his sock and shoe back on. After she sat down, he got up and got in line with another class that was leaving the lunchroom. Jonathan sat down and moved his feet as if running in place. He stood up, went over to another table, and kissed another child. He returned to his seat. He got up again and ran to the door. He was stopped by his teacher and returned to his seat.

The Stanford Binet Intelligence Scale, Form L-M was attempted. No base-line age was obtained because Jonathan was unable to correctly demonstrate two skills at the two-year level. Jonathan was able to successfully demonstrate some skills through the three year, six-month level. Highest successes were in visual-motor skills. He was unable to successfully demonstrate any expressive language skills. Jonathan's performance on this test indicates that he is performing significantly below expected levels in all areas. Jonathan was able to successfully demonstrate non-verbal skills through the 30-month level. However, he was unable to demonstrate language skills above the 17-month level.

I always dreaded those reports, even though I knew they were necessary in order to formulate the best plan for Jonathan. Some days I could hardly stand it. I sat and tried to capture the memories of him before he became sick.

However, he *was* making progress, even though it was very slow and difficult to see. We constantly searched for any signs of improvement. One particular evening, I sat down to relax after dinner. Out of the clear blue, Jonathan stood up and blurted out, "You have to call the right doctor." He then turned around, sat back down, and resumed playing with a toy.

Excitement coursed through my veins. I jumped up and shouted for Johnny to come quickly. "Jonathan, tell Daddy what you just said."

"You have to call the right doctor," he repeated. We couldn't believe it. He rarely spoke sentences that long. We had been praying for months for a miracle. I looked at Johnny. "Maybe he's trying to tell us something. Maybe we just haven't found the right doctor yet." My adrenaline level shot up several notches.

A few days later, while watching television together, a commercial came on promoting a local medical center. Guess what the ad said? "You have to call the right doctor." Jonathan had heard that ad sometime in the past, and somehow it had stuck in his brain. It became a favorite phrase of his and a source of laughter for us every time he said it.

We hit a major milestone in November of 1984. Home IV nutrition had kept Jonathan alive for the previous two years. For months, we had been working with a nutritionist. Once a month we submitted to her a list of *everything* that he consumed orally. He needed 1800 calories per day before we could even consider stopping his IV feeding. We measured and recorded everything he ate and drank. The nutritionist keyed the information into her computer, which produced a printout of his calorie intake and vitamin breakdown. Her report determined if he'd had an adequate intake of protein, carbohydrates, and fats as well as calories.

Month after month, we submitted the information, and month after month, we received the discouraging news that though he had begun to eat *something* at each meal, his intake did not meet his nutritional needs. Finally, in November, we received the long-awaited call from his gastrointestinal doctor. He had evaluated the latest report from the nutritionist, and they both agreed that we could stop his home IV therapy. Yea! We circled up and did the happy dance. It was a huge step in the right direction, and we thanked God for the miracle.

Chapter 29

New School and Return to Disney World

The school psychologist and Jonathan's teacher wanted to transfer Jonathan to a safer environment because of his tendency to run away and his lack of judgment when running. They asked Johnny and me to visit a special education center located in our county called Rose Garden. Though part of the public school system, the entire population of Rose Garden consisted of mentally and/or physically disabled students. Johnny and I had never heard of the school but agreed to check it out. Not wanting to take Jonathan with us on the first visit, we drove to Rose Garden one day during Jonathan's school day.

I don't know if I have the words to describe my first impression of Rose Garden. Jonathan and Jamie had always attended schools immaculately landscaped, architecturally appealing, and relatively new. Without even realizing it, I had become a snob. Rose Garden was none of the above, and, to be honest, I couldn't imagine my child attending school there. The building looked old and unattractive—probably dating back to the 1940s—and sat in the middle of a poor, rundown neighborhood. A 10-foot high fence surrounded the entire school. It looked more like a prison than a school. Jonathan definitely would not escape from that place.

As we approached the building, we heard rock music blaring loudly from a boom box. About fifteen older students were out on the playground dancing vigorously to the music. I had to admit, they looked like they were having the time of their lives. They were laughing and talking back and forth to one another. Most of the students had Down syndrome; a few occupied wheelchairs. I know this is a strange statement, but to me, they all just looked *so* handicapped. I'm ashamed to admit this, but before Jonathan became handicapped, I didn't know a single disabled person. Not one. It wasn't that I lacked compassion or understanding; I had just not given disabled individuals much thought. And even though Jonathan had been in a class for the disabled for the previous two years, my mind still had difficulty comprehending that he, too, was handicapped.

Before we even got out of the car, I turned to Johnny and attempted to explain how I felt, "Jonathan does not belong with these kids. He is not like them. He belongs with 'normal' kids." I began to cry softly. "Do we have to go in? Can't we just leave now and let him stay where he is?"

"Louise, no one understands better than I how hard this is. However, for Jonathan's sake, we have to accept the fact that he *is* like these kids—he *is* handicapped. We need to go in and see what the school is like and at least give it a chance."

I knew he was right. My emotions fluctuated daily between acceptance and denial. We went in and introduced ourselves to the principal, who was expecting us. She graciously took us on a tour of the building and introduced us to all the teachers. Everyone appeared to be happy—teachers and students alike. We observed a physical education class in progress in the gym. We watched for a while and were amazed at how well the teacher had geared all the activities to the students' level of functioning.

We discovered that physical therapy, occupational therapy, and speech therapy were available to all students at Rose Garden who needed that type of assistance. Additionally, learning that all teachers and teacher's aides received training and certification in

CPR and first aid convinced me that Rose Garden would provide a safe environment for Jonathan. They were all familiar with seizures and knew how to respond. I could feel myself gradually softening towards Rose Garden. The school felt more like a big family than a public school.

At home, we prayed for wisdom and asked God to give us direction and peace about Jonathan's school placement. In the meantime, Jonathan's current teacher asked for our permission to take him to Rose Garden for a visit during school hours. As they were walking from class to class meeting the Rose Garden teachers, Jonathan poked his head into one classroom and gave the teacher his finest smile. The teacher, Shirley Camp, later told me, "I loved Jonathan the first moment I laid eyes on him. I knew if he came to Rose Garden I would fight to have him in my class."

In April of 1985, Jonathan transferred to Rose Garden into Shirley's class. The night before Jonathan began attending Rose Garden Shirley called me at home. "I just want you and Johnny to know how very excited I am to be able to work with Jonathan and watch him learn. I would appreciate it if you would remember to pray for me each day."

She didn't even have to ask. Despite our earlier trepidation, we knew that Rose Garden provided the safest environment for Jonathan and Shirley's class the perfect placement.

Shirley immediately began working with Jonathan on reading simple words and sentences, identifying body parts, reciting the days of the week and months of the year, and learning personal information such as name, address, and telephone number. She used every creative method imaginable—role playing, puppet shows, tea parties, pretend trips to the grocery store—anything and everything she could think of to help him relearn. It became her goal in life to help him make a complete recovery. Sometimes we couldn't tell who was more excited when he made progress, Johnny and me, Shirley, or Barbara, Shirley's paraprofessional. On one occasion, Shirley had Johnny and me sneak into her classroom and hide in a huge cardboard box so that we could witness first-hand his latest discovery.

One day at school, Shirley utilized a string puppet named Jolly Jack and a toy car to teach the children, especially Jonathan, the importance of crossing the street safely and not running into the street. We enjoyed a good laugh when we read the note she sent home that day. "I'm not sure how effective the safety lesson was today," she wrote. "Jonathan laughed hysterically when Jolly Jack got knocked down by the car."

I had never known a teacher as gifted as Shirley or a more compassionate and loving paraprofessional than Barbara. They made an awesome team, and they genuinely loved Jonathan. All the fears I had experienced about Rose Garden melted away completely. Thankfully, God doesn't always give us what we ask for, but instead, gives us what we need.

The month of May brought an unexpected surprise for the students at Rose Garden. A new foundation in Atlanta that granted wishes to disabled and terminally ill children heard about the students at Rose Garden and wanted to do something special for them. As a "kick off" and media blitz, the foundation offered to fly all of the children from Rose Garden and another special school to Disney World for the day. I couldn't imagine a more daunting task. Because of Jonathan's habit of running away, they allowed both Johnny and me to accompany him. We were excited about going, but we couldn't help remembering that it had been at Disney World, less than four years earlier, when his medical problems had begun. Would he remember having been there?

The long anticipated day finally arrived. While most of Atlanta lay sleeping, 125 excited children with varying degrees of physical and mental impairments gathered at the Atlanta airport early on a Saturday morning. Seventy-five anxious parents and numerous volunteers accompanied them. Many of the children had never flown on an airplane or even been away from home for an entire day. The parents stood by anxiously biting their nails and downing gallons of coffee while waiting to board the plane.

Just loading the chartered jet required a lot of patience. The local Jaycees and police officers who had volunteered to help formed a line from the bottom of the steps all the way to the entrance of the plane to assist (or carry if necessary) each child to his seat. Those who were able to walk boarded first, then wheelchair-bound students. An hour-and-a-half later, we could feel the excitement among the students as the plane readied for takeoff. A spontaneous round of applause and whoops of excitement broke out as the plane lifted into the air.

Once we reached our destination, everyone had to transfer to awaiting buses for the trip to Disney World. Finally, we all arrived at the park. Each person received a special pass that allowed him or her to proceed to a private entrance at the front of the line for each ride. Jonathan loved the rides and the excitement of the day, but gave no evidence that he remembered his previous visit. We had suspected that his memory was impaired, but it had been difficult to determine because of his limited verbal skills.

We flew through the park cramming as much fun into the five hours we spent at Disney World as possible. Then, tired and weary, everyone headed back to the airport for the journey home. Happy sighs and occasional snoring replaced the noise and excitement of the morning trip. It had been a day that would not soon be forgotten.

Chapter 30

Gradual Progress

Jonathan continued to make such good progress under Shirley's tutelage that she offered to work with him a couple of days a week during the summer at her home. I readily said "yes" because it would help him to retain what he had learned, and it would give me some time alone with Jamie.

Shirley had a natural ability for turning every situation into a teaching opportunity. Jonathan and Shirley took walks in the neighborhood and counted mailboxes. They practiced walking slowly, and they talked about the importance of not running away. The two of them made trips to the supermarket and identified items on the shelves. Their excursions were never boring. Jonathan's sentences continued to be inappropriate occasionally. One day in the supermarket, Jonathan saw a girl who resembled Jamie and startled everyone around him, especially the girl, when he yelled, "Stop! I want to kiss you!"

Shirley continued trying to teach Jonathan to read. One day he successfully read from a book, "I love mom. I love dad." Suddenly, he looked up from the book and shouted, "Let us all love one another." It sounded like an excerpt from a sermon lodged somewhere in his memory bank.

During another teaching session Shirley asked him, "Jonathan, where is Daddy?"

"At work," he replied.

"Where is Jamie?"

"At home," he correctly answered.

"Where is Mommy?"

Without missing a beat he exclaimed, "Mommy ran away." There were still days when I longed to do just that.

During the summer of 1985, the house next door to us came up for sale. My parents had considered moving to Marietta in order to help us with Jonathan. They decided to purchase the house next door. Mother had lost most of her vision because of diabetes. She could no longer drive, and she needed help shopping for groceries and clothes. It gave us an opportunity to help her, and they were a tremendous help to us with Jonathan. Jamie especially loved having them next door. She and her grandpa were frequent diners at the local pancake house and pizza parlor.

When school began again in the fall, we were thrilled that Jonathan was able to stay in Shirley and Barbara's class. Because he had worked with Shirley during the summer, we didn't have to endure a time of adjustment. He especially loved his physical education class, and it gave him a legitimate opportunity to release pent-up energy.

Jonathan had excellent eye/hand coordination and could follow directions about half of the time, but he remained impulsive and easily frustrated when corrected or when he didn't get his way. He also had difficulty waiting his turn. One day when told he couldn't jump on the trampoline in the gym, he demonstrated his displeasure by removing all of his clothes.

He loved the playground outdoors, particularly the swings and slide. Shirley often used the playground as a reward for good behavior. On one occasion, he played so hard that his ostomy bag began to come loose. When he saw that it was leaking onto his underwear, he walked over to Shirley and announced appropriately, "I've got a problem."

His vocabulary steadily improved. He learned to recite the entire Pledge of Allegiance perfectly, and he loved to sing. At the annual Rose Garden talent show that year, he stood on the stage and sang "Jesus Loves Me" and "It's a Small World." We were encouraged that he remembered the words to songs that he had known before the stroke. We even discovered that he relearned information faster if we sang it to him. It sounded rather stupid, I'm sure, to an outsider, but we sang phrases like, "we eat with a spoon and fork," or "we drink our milk from a cup."

One day he came home from school and asked, "Mommy, is it Rose Reagan?"

I said, "Do you mean Ronald Reagan?" When he said "yes," I called Shirley to see if they had discussed Ronald Reagan that day. Her answer surprised me. She said the news had been on during the students' naptime, and the newscaster had been discussing Ronald Reagan's upcoming trip to Atlanta. Apparently, Jonathan even learned while sleeping.

On another occasion, Jonathan's class joined the class next door to watch a movie. A child from the other class began making noise and acting out. His teacher said, "I'm going to make you leave the room if you can't behave." Jonathan yelled, "Yeah, kick him out!" They were probably thinking his vocabulary had progressed far enough. He, on the other hand was probably glad not to be occupying the "naughty seat" for once.

We had discovered only two types of discipline that seemed effective with Jonathan. One was time out. One day after he ran away from Shirley in the hall, she said, "Jonathan, go put yourself in time out." Amazingly, he went straight to his classroom, opened the door, and sat down in the time-out chair.

The other form of discipline was unusual and somewhat controversial. His previous teacher, a graduate student at Georgia State University, with our permission, discussed Jonathan's behavior with her psychology professor. He recommended that we try a discipline method that had proven to be very effective and completely pain-free. It had been especially effective with children like Jonathan who had very limited reasoning ability. It involved spraying the child with cold water to stop negative behavior. She explained that it was a radical approach and would require that everyone working with Jonathan agree to implement it.

We were ready to try almost anything to improve Jonathan's behavior. We gave our permission and agreed to use the technique at home as well. I bought several small travel-sized hairspray bottles and filled them with water. We carried them everywhere we went and used them discreetly whenever necessary. I discovered that they were small enough to fit in a pocket or slide under a sweater cuff. He absolutely hated it, but we began to see improvement in his behavior. We were gradually able to phase out the use of the water bottles, but for years afterwards, we only had to say, "do you want me to spray you?" and his behavior changed abruptly for the better.

Chapter 31

Grandparents in Time-Out

Jonathan's level of comprehension, though far from normal, continued to improve. One Saturday morning as Johnny worked in the backyard, he realized he needed something in the house. Finding the back door locked, he began knocking on the door. Jonathan walked into our bedroom, got me by the hand, led me to the back door, and simply said, "Daddy." His ability to recognize that Johnny needed my help, to come and get me, and to take me to where he had seen Johnny knocking at the door represented a huge step in his thinking ability.

Another day he led me to the back door and simply said, "swing." Johnny had built him a sturdy swing between two huge trees in the backyard. It had become a favorite pastime. Whenever he found the words to verbalize a need or desire, we moved heaven and earth to fulfill his request in order to help reinforce good reasoning skills.

We discovered the hard way that the back yard held great fascination for Jonathan. Once when Johnny's parents were visiting, I had to take Jamie to a doctor's appointment. Johnny was at work, and my parents had come over from next door. All four grandparents were sitting around the table in the kitchen visiting with each other. They insisted that I leave Jonathan with them while I took Jamie to the doctor. Daddy must have sensed my reluctance. "I think four mature adults can handle one little boy, Louise," he insisted. "Go on; he'll be fine." It certainly sounded logical. Jamie and I headed out the door.

Some time had passed with the grandparents talking and catching up on each other's lives, when it suddenly dawned on them that Jonathan was not in the room. Frantically, they began searching the house, to no avail. Looking out the window, they spotted him in the backyard swinging with a broad smile on his face. They were stunned. We had installed locks that were too high for him to reach at the top of all doors leading outside. Jamie and I had checked them before we left. However, the lock on the door leading to the backyard had definitely been unfastened. Apparently, Jonathan had moved an ottoman to the back door, climbed up on the ottoman, unlocked the door, pushed the ottoman back to where it came from (so no one would suspect he had moved it), and shut the door behind him. He had carefully planned his escape. We didn't know whether to be proud of his ability to think that through, or to be angry that something terrible could have happened to him. We seriously considered putting the grandparents in "time-out" for negligence.

We were very aware that his level of comprehension and his expressive and receptive language skills were still extremely impaired, but we were thankful for every new word and every sign of improvement. According to most doctors, improvement following a stroke only occurred during the first six months. Yet, Jonathan continued to learn new words and phrases.

The spiritual training Jonathan had received from birth often emerged in unexpected ways. Shirley and Barbara, his schoolteachers, had always said a blessing with their students before lunch. One day they were busy opening lunch boxes and helping everyone at the table get ready to eat and had not yet gotten around to saying the blessing. Jonathan got tired of waiting, bowed his head, shouted "amen," and commenced to eat.

When legislators passed laws prohibiting prayer in school, the teachers at Rose Garden attempted to comply. Explaining the ruling to the mentally disabled students at Rose Garden, however, was next to impossible. The first day the new law took effect, Shirley and Barbara placed the students' lunches in front of them and instructed them to begin eating. The students sat very still with their hands in their laps wearing blank expressions. Shirley tried again. "Go ahead and eat." They continued to sit staring at Shirley and Barbara, refusing to eat until someone voiced a prayer. Finally, in desperation, Shirley said, "To heck with the law. Bow your heads and let's pray." Once the students thanked God for their food, they all immediately began to eat.

At the age of five, shortly before Jonathan had become sick, he had begun to ask numerous spiritual questions. One day with no prodding, Jonathan asked me, "Mommy, where is God?" We talked about God being in heaven and in his heart. We never knew how much he understood. "How does Jesus come to live in my heart?" "How do I give my heart to Jesus?" "What does it mean to be a Christian?" We attempted to answer his questions as simply as possible because of his young age. We explained that receiving Jesus as your Savior was the most important decision he would ever make in life. Jesus would be his best friend forever, and he could talk to Jesus about anything and everything. And that Jesus would talk to him through His Word, the Bible. We weren't surprised when at the tender age of five he told us he was ready to give his heart to Jesus. He wanted to make public his decision to receive Christ during our church service, but we encouraged him to wait a little while longer because of his young age. In the meantime, we continued to talk to him about what it meant to be a Christian. I regret very much not allowing him to make his decision publicly. Not because it changed what was in his heart. Not at all. But because it prevented us and others from seeing him declare publicly what he had decided privately.

Chapter 32

Goodbye Charlie

In March 1986 Jonathan participated in Special Olympics for the first time. Since he loved running so much, we decided what better event than a relay race. The day of the event dawned sunny and warm. Anticipation and excitement perfectly described our mood. Johnny's parents had come to Atlanta for the big event. They, along with my parents and the four of us, found our way to our assigned area. Enthusiastic, boisterous fans packed the bleachers. Families waved banners and shouted cheers for their athletes. The mood was contagious. Everyone came armed with cameras, binoculars and snacks.

Jamie had volunteered to be a "catcher" for Jonathan's event. Her job involved standing at the finish line, catching Jonathan when he completed the race, and giving him a huge hug. Each participant had a designated catcher assigned to him. As we expected, Jonathan ran like the wind during his race, leaving everyone in his dust. He won the first of many gold medals that day.

Johnny and I celebrated our twentieth wedding anniversary in May. With my parents next door and Jamie completing her junior year in high school, we felt comfortable leaving Jonathan for a few days and taking a long-overdue trip, just the two of us. We flew to Cancun, Mexico to soak up the sun, tour ancient ruins, and just relax. Phone calls from Mexico were very expensive, so we informed Jamie and my parents to call us *only* in the event of an emergency. Otherwise, we would contact them when we had a layover in Houston on our way home.

We had a marvelous time and didn't hear from them, so we assumed everything had gone well. Still, the mother instinct in me was screaming loudly by the time we landed in Houston. I hurried to the pay phone. Jamie answered and assured us Jonathan was fine. "As a matter of fact, he has been eating really well ever since we got back from the emergency room," she calmly volunteered.

"EMERGENCY ROOM!" My heart fell to my stomach. "Why was he in the emergency room? Why didn't you call us?" I asked. I mentally vowed never to leave town again. Actually, the emergency room visit turned out to be only precautionary. The school nurse had taken Jonathan's blood pressure and had noticed that it registered a little high. Knowing that we were out of town, she had called my parents, and just to be on the safe side, they had decided to take him to the emergency room to have it checked again. Jonathan was fine, and it was simply a false alarm. I whispered a prayer of thanksgiving that we didn't know about that until our trip had ended, or we would certainly have come home early.

The summer of 1986 brought the best news we had received from Jonathan's doctors in a long time. They all agreed that he was well enough to close off his ileostomy. Goodbye "Charlie"! "Charlie" had not been a great deal of trouble before Jonathan's stroke, but he had been a royal pain in the neck since his stroke.

We gathered our prayer warriors together to pray that there would be no complications before, during, or after the surgery. We also prayed that the surgery would be successful. Jonathan had had the ileostomy for four long years. Because of his mental state and inability to reason, the doctors were not sure if he would be able to control his bowel functions or if he would need to be potty trained all over again. If the operation failed, we would have to return to surgery to bring "Charlie" back. No one wanted that.

Thankfully, his surgery was a complete success. After a week recuperating in the hospital, Jonathan came home. The doctors instructed us that for the first few weeks his system would be adjusting to the change. That proved to be an understatement. He had terrible diarrhea, and because he had not had a normal bowel movement for four years, his bottom became irritated and raw. He spent the first week at home soaking in warm water with Epsom salts. Gradually, over several months, the situation improved, and he regained total bowel control.

My parents had joined a small church near our home not long after they moved next door. Fortunately for us, their church had a small special needs class for handicapped children. My dad insisted on taking Jonathan with them in order for Johnny, Jamie, and me to be able to attend our church together. For the past three years, Johnny and I had taken turns attending church. One Sunday Johnny would attend the morning service while I stayed home with Jonathan, and I would attend the evening service. The next week we would reverse the schedule. We had always attended as a family, and this arrangement had been difficult for all of us. We missed worshipping together. Though we were thankful that Jonathan could attend the special needs class at my parents' church, we knew that our home church needed to provide that type of ministry to other families in our community. Johnny sought our pastor's help. He agreed to assist us with beginning a special needs ministry at our church, if we could locate a qualified person to teach the class.

Not too long after his talk with our pastor, Johnny came home from church so excited. "You'll never guess what happened in Sunday school today." He proceeded to share with me that a couple had been visiting our class who were former members. They had recently moved back to Marietta from North Carolina.

While sharing prayer requests, Johnny had asked the class to pray about our desire to establish a special needs ministry at our church and our need for a qualified person to lead the ministry. The visitor, Linda Baker, spoke up volunteering, "I have a background in special education and would love to teach the class. I'll call your wife next week to set up a time to meet Jonathan." WOW! Sometimes we pray and pray and think God must be hard of hearing, and then He suddenly blows us away with His answer.

Linda proved true to her word. The next week, she and her daughter, Jill, came to our house to meet Jonathan. They both had an instant rapport with him and were not the least bit intimated by his extensive medical history.

Linda began our special needs ministry in our home, since Jonathan was the first and only class member. She and Jill came every Sunday and had class with Jonathan while we went to church.

In January of 1987, Linda held a meeting at our church for potential helpers for our new class. We weren't sure if anyone would show up. You can only imagine our complete shock when eighteen people came to the meeting or expressed an interest in helping. Most of them had never worked with handicapped children before, and they were admittedly terrified at the prospect. However, they were willing to learn, and a willing spirit was the most important requirement.

Linda conducted several training sessions for the volunteers, and soon afterwards, the church assigned our class their own Sunday school room with a private bathroom attached. We moved the Special Gift's Class from our home to the church.

Linda placed announcements in our church newsletter promoting our new ministry. Before we knew it, we had seven members ranging in age from seven to thirty-one. Linda and Jill continued to teach the class using Sunday school literature designed especially for special needs students. They incorporated music, arts, crafts, puzzles, and story-time to teach the children Bible truths about Jesus. We had frequent birthday parties, bowling outings, and the largest Christmas extravaganza imaginable.

The students were thrilled when a couple of years after Linda began the class, the local newspaper devoted half a page to a story featuring our Special Gift's class. They all strutted around like celebrities, offering to give autographs to any takers.

The close of the 1986/'87 school year came quickly. Jonathan underwent extensive testing by the school psychologist, and she branded him with a new label: Severely Mentally Handicapped. Though a difficult pill to swallow, I knew in the deep recesses of my heart that it was accurate. He tested low in all areas, but especially in abstract reasoning and his ability to understand spoken language. He scored no higher than three years old in every area except socialization. A born extrovert, regardless of what he had been through medically, his social skills were his greatest gift from God.

Instead of dwelling on Jonathan's disabilities, I turned my focus that spring to an exciting event taking place in our family: Jamie's graduation from high school. It's difficult to put into words how proud we were of her. Our family had experienced so much turmoil throughout her entire high school years, yet she graduated with a 4.26 grade point average on a 4.0 scale. (She achieved higher than a 4.0 by taking advanced placement classes.) She graduated valedictorian out of almost 500 in her class. She had never made less than an "A" in any class throughout all four years of high school. I know I'm bragging shamelessly, but when I think back to our abnormal lifestyle, I honestly don't think it would have been possible to accomplish that except for the prayer she had prayed her freshmen year asking God to allow her to graduate as the class valedictorian. God had instilled in her a desire for excellence.

The Bible states in I Corinthians 10:31b, "Whatever you do, do all to the glory of God." Jamie took that verse to heart. I remember a friend asking one time how we instilled such good study habits in Jamie. I laughed and replied, "We never encouraged her to study. As a matter of fact, we sometimes begged her to stop." She took so many advanced courses her senior year, she often studied way into the night, and a few times pulled all-nighters. We couldn't wait for her to graduate so we could all get a good night's sleep.

As she stood on the stage during her graduation ceremony and spoke to the huge crowd gathered for the event, I wondered how different her life would have been if Jonathan had never been ill. Would she have excelled academically? Would she have become a "woman after God's own heart?" She spoke that day on the importance of setting goals, on visualizing your dreams and working hard to achieve them, and on seeking God's wisdom and guidance throughout your life.

She would be leaving the nest and heading to college in the fall. We prayed that she would continue to strive for academic excellence, but even more importantly, that she would continue to grow and mature in her walk with the Lord.

Chapter 33

Very Special Friends

As our fledgling Sunday school class began to grow, Jonathan's circle of friends expanded also. Each new member came with his or her own special personality and uniqueness. Soon after our Special Gift's Class found its home at our church, I asked Shirley if she would allow her son, Flint, to attend. She readily agreed. Flint, who has Down syndrome, had been adopted by Shirley and Bill at five years of age. God could not have found better parents for Flint. Unable to have children of their own, they loved him and spoiled him with a passion. I had never met anyone as delightful, interesting, and entertaining as Flint. Because he attended Jonathan's school and Jonathan spent so much time at Shirley's house, Flint became like a member of our family. Though limited in some ways, Flint possessed many gifts that offset any limitations he may have had.

Flint loved tools. On one occasion, he took his dad's screwdriver and proceeded to remove every doorknob in their house. There was only one problem: he couldn't remember how to reverse the process.

Another time he became angry with his mom because she wouldn't allow him to do something he wanted to do. Though unable to read or write, he grabbed a notebook and a pen and dashed out the door. He canvassed the entire neighborhood for the next hour imploring them to sign his petition to move to his own apartment. The neighbors were all well acquainted with Flint and decided to humor him. He returned home with a page full of signatures and couldn't understand why Shirley would not allow him to move into his own apartment.

Shirley dreaded salespeople calling on the phone when she was outside or unable to answer. Flint answered the phone on one such occasion and it happened to be an overly zealous magazine salesman soliciting subscriptions. Before Shirley realized what had transpired, her mailbox overflowed with practically every magazine in print.

When Flint was somewhere around seven or eight years old, Shirley took him along on a shopping excursion to a department store. While Shirley paid for her purchase, she observed a treasured encounter between Flint and a mannequin. Flint had no idea that the mannequin was not a real person. Remembering his lessons to always be polite to people he encountered, he approached the mannequin with a wide smile on his face and his right hand extended. "Hi, how are you?" he said, warmly greeting the plastic dummy. When the mannequin made no response, he tried again. "Hi, how are you doing?" Still no response. Becoming somewhat exasperated, he decided to give it one more attempt. "Hi, how are you today?" Silence. By that time, Flint had had it with that rude "person." In anger and disgust, he verbally lashed out at the mannequin as he stomped off towards his mom, "Well fine. Don't speak to me then. See if I care."

Flint loved television, especially sit-coms. One time when the characters on a favorite program moved to California, Flint promptly stuffed all his clothes in his suitcase and headed out the door. Shirley chased after him and questioned him, "Where in the world do you think you're going with that suitcase, Flint?" He rolled his eyes and replied with a great deal of exasperation and drama, "Mom, I have to go to California. All my television friends are moving there!"

A few months after Jamie left for college, we invited Flint to spend the weekend with us. Shirley and Bill were taking a long-overdue weekend trip, and we looked forward to having Flint visit. We told him he could stay in "the sister's" room (his name for Jamie). His arrival completely threw us off guard.

Our jaws dropped wide open when Flint and his parents began to unload his stuff from their car. Not only had he brought his own huge television and separate VCR machine, but he had also unloaded an enormous boom box, a bulging briefcase filled with his "papers," and a huge suitcase with clothing spilling out all sides. "Uh, how long did you say you would be gone?" I tentatively asked Shirley.

As soon as they drove away, Flint set to work in Jamie's room. With the door closed and instructions for us not to enter until he finished unpacking, he went to work, and we left him on his own. We were becoming a little concerned with how long he had been behind that closed door when he finally emerged with a look of triumph on his face. "You can come in and see *my* room now," he exclaimed, grinning from ear to ear. We were shocked at the transformation. He had completely rearranged everything in the room. He had relocated all the furniture and removed everything Jamie had carefully placed on her walls—pictures of her friends, high school banners, nick-knacks, everything—and had replaced them with his own pictures and posters. Daisy Duke stared back at us as well as the Fonz and the Hulk. We were speechless. Jamie would have had a heart attack if she had walked in unexpectedly. Flint really took to heart "moving in." We had a delightful weekend and then managed to restore the room to its original state so that Jamie was none the wiser.

Dominique joined our Special Gifts class soon after Flint. "Nikki," as we all came to call her, had been born with cerebral palsy. Confined to a wheelchair and unable to speak, Nikki always sported the most fashionable outfits, jewelry, and shoes. We treasured her sweet personality. A persistent smile graced her pretty face, and she never met a stranger. I'm convinced that even though she was unable to communicate verbally, Nikki understood everything spoken to her. Her facial expressions and body language suggested an intelligence that her body belied.

Our little Sunday school class was well underway when Allyson joined. Extremely friendly and outgoing, Allyson approached everyone with her arms outstretched, ready to embrace them in a hug. Only mildly mentally disabled, Allyson could read on an elementary school level and possessed many other gifts as well. God had given her a love of music and the ability to sing with a radiant, rich voice. She often sang for other Sunday school classes and captivated them with her voice and her message of God's love. Allyson later went on to record her very own CD.

In addition to singing, Allyson showed a real entrepreneurial spirit by creating her own line of beautiful beaded jewelry. She also developed her own computer greeting card company, and she sold Avon products. We may have to form a line to borrow money from Allyson one of these days.

My purpose in introducing you to these "special" friends is two-fold. First, never think for one minute that Sunday school time and space is wasted on these precious people. Each person in our class is capable of learning about God on some level, and it would not surprise me at all to learn that they have a much greater capacity for loving God than the rest of us. They are often much more attentive and receptive than many "normal" adults. Allyson can read and comprehend children's Bible stories. Nikki listens attentively. Flint ushers you to the very throne of God when he prays. He is wondrously child-like as he loudly petitions God on behalf of everyone he knows including Santa Claus and the Easter Bunny. In addition, Jonathan, whose mental capabilities are very limited, has the ability to memorize and retain God's Word. He never goes to sleep at night without reciting five Bible verses complete with references:

John 3:16: "For God so loved the world that He gave His only begotten Son, that whoever believes in Him should not perish but have everlasting life."

Psalm 118:24: "This is the day which the Lord has made; we will rejoice and be glad in it."

Philippians 4:13: "I can do all things through Christ who strengthens me."

Genesis 1:1: "In the beginning God created the heavens and the earth."

Psalm 119:105: "Your word is a lamp to my feet and a light to my path."

Jesus said in Matthew 18:3, "Assuredly, I say to you, unless you are converted and become as little children, you will by no means enter the kingdom of heaven." In addition, in Matthew 19:14, He said, "Let the little children come to Me, and do not forbid them; for of such is the kingdom of heaven." Just like Flint, Nikki, Allyson, and Jonathan, we need to come to Jesus with faith that is pure and simple.

My second purpose in helping you become acquainted with these special friends is to illustrate the unique talents and personalities God has given to each of them. I hope you can sense how precious they are to God. In Psalm 139:13-14 God's Word states, "For You have formed my inward parts; You have covered me in my mother's womb. I will praise You, for I am fearfully and wonderfully made." Psalm 119:73a reveals, "Your hands have made me and fashioned me"

Every life is precious in God's eyes, and we can learn much from these special people. By showing unconditional love and acceptance of these unique people, we demonstrate a picture of God's unconditional love for us. I wish everyone could meet Flint, Nikki, Allyson, and Jonathan. A friend once said to me, "What if, when we get to heaven, we realize that they were actually "normal" and we were the ones who were disabled." That is definitely food for thought.

Chapter 34

The Grinch Who Stole Christmas

The following years brought many changes for Jonathan. He had several different teachers at Rose Garden, and Shirley continued to work with him during the summers. Special education students were encouraged to spend time each week during their regular school day in the community participating in a job-training program. Most of the students had job training one or two days a week for three or four hours. Though unpaid while on a training program, the special instruction with a job coach allowed many students to find employment at a job that matched their skills when they finished high school. For Jonathan, each new school year included a new job in the community. One year he worked at a supermarket operating the box crusher. That simply involved pushing a button. The machine made a tremendous amount of noise while it gobbled up the boxes. Naturally, Jonathan loved it.

Another year he had a job at a local hospital packaging plastic spoons, forks, and knives for patients' trays. He loved the repetitive nature of the job but hated to wear the gloves that the job required.

Another interesting job took place at a local hotel. Jonathan and his classmates were responsible for cleaning one of the guest rooms. They dusted, vacuumed, and changed the sheets. Even though they were required to wear gloves, I worried about germs and potential diseases. Jonathan never became sick, but a different dilemma accompanied that occupation. He enjoyed stripping the beds so much that he decided that would be a fun activity at home as well.

The funniest job he had was at a pet store. The job required that he take cans of cat food out of a large box and place them on the store shelf. That seemed like the perfect job for Jonathan. He had exhibited a great deal of obsessive/compulsive behaviors and loved for everything to be orderly. One problem quickly arose, however. Johnny and Jamie had always been very allergic to cats, so we had never owned one for a pet. I don't know if for some reason Jonathan didn't like cats, or if he just wasn't accustomed to being around them. Whatever the reason, every time he put a can of cat food on the shelf, he methodically turned the picture of the cat towards the back of the shelf so the customer could not see the picture. Of course, the store manager wanted the picture of the cat facing the customer. No amount of discussion could dissuade Jonathan from doing it his way. Needless to say, he didn't last long at that job.

Every year at Christmas, Rose Garden presented a play for the parents and the community. The handicapped students performed the entire play, and it always proved to be entertaining as well as predictably unpredictable. It was a festive occasion that involved as many students as possible. Our entire family became involved. Johnny posed as Santa Claus, and Jamie dressed as an elf and assisted students distributing programs.

One particular year the students performed *The Grinch Who Stole Christmas*. Jonathan loved to grimace and make faces at everyone, which made him a perfect fit for the Grinch. A narrator, usually one of the teachers, read the story, and the students acted out their parts and provided sound effects. Jonathan carried out his role perfectly, baring his teeth and making weird faces and mouth noises at the audience. He had the entire crowd in stitches.

Jonathan continued to enjoy participating in Special Olympics. In 1990 he branched out to train in swimming, bowling, and horseback riding. My parents, who lived next door to us, had an in-ground swimming pool. We sensed an urgency for Jonathan to learn to swim in the event that he wandered over to their back yard undetected. I am so grateful for the Special Olympics program and the scores of faithful volunteers who freely gave of their time each week. They patiently worked with Jonathan until he could successfully swim from one end of the pool to the other. He took like a duck to "splashing in the water," his term for swimming. His seizure disorder prevented him from swimming alone and required that he participate in Developmental Special Olympics activities. All athletes in the developmental program are required to have a volunteer with them at all times, in the event that a seizure or other medical situation should occur. That meant that Jonathan always had a volunteer in the water swimming right alongside him.

He has accumulated gold, silver, and bronze medals in state competition developmental swimming, but the color of the medal makes no difference to him whatsoever. Furthermore, whether he wins or loses is totally meaningless to him. The only thing he cares about is "splashing in the water." And that's the way it should be.

Bowling is the same way. The minute we walk into a bowling alley, Jonathan gets so excited he can hardly wait to begin. It's interesting to watch him in action. He doesn't look at the pins; he doesn't aim. He simply walks to the stopping point, bends slightly at the waist, and throws the ball. He quite often scores a strike or spare. I've tried to watch and learn from him since I've been officially voted by our Sunday school class as the worst bowler in the class (and I have a trophy to prove it), but Jonathan consistently out-scores me.

Horseback riding was another story. Jonathan didn't appear to be afraid of the horse, but he never completely comprehended the competition rules. He primarily loved the attention he received from the volunteers. In developmental horseback riding, three volunteers are required per athlete, one on each side of the horse, and another in front to lead the horse. Of course, all three volunteers were cute high school girls who bragged on him and encouraged him. He basked in all the attention he received from them as much as he loved the activity itself.

Jonathan also joined a Challenger Little League baseball team during the summer. What a great concept. The adult coaches paired special needs kids with "buddies" from regular Little League teams. The buddies stayed right alongside the special needs players helping them bat, catch, and run the bases. Jonathan's first time at bat, he hit the ball, but it apparently didn't go as far as he had envisioned. He quickly ran forward, retrieved the ball, and threw it as far as he could; then he ran like the wind. The Challenger team proved more entertaining than the Atlanta Braves!

At the end of the 1990/91 school year, Jonathan's teacher and the principal determined he would benefit from a special education class in a regular school setting—the middle school only a mile from our house. His behavior had improved, and his running episodes had become rare events. We had all grown to love Rose Garden and its family atmosphere. The thought of changing schools sent terror through my heart. I loved the idea of having him in a school so close to home, but I worried about how he would fare with regular students. He had been "secluded" for over five years at Rose Garden, attending school exclusively with disabled students.

I scheduled a meeting with his new teacher a few days before the school year began, and my apprehensions completely vanished. Very professional and loaded with personality, she connected with Jonathan and him with her right from the start.

The end of the 1991 school year provided a transition for Jamie as well. Since she had graduated from college with a major in biology, everyone who knew her asked if she planned to study medicine. She always responded with a resounding "No!" Jonathan's multiple health issues had exposed our family to every area of medicine at one time or another. Jamie had seen enough for a lifetime. We never pushed her towards or away from medicine. We simply continued to pray for God's wisdom and for God to reveal His perfect plan for her life.

Something changed during her junior year. She decided to join the pre-med society on campus and explore the possibility of medicine. She also conferred with Jonathan's doctor, who provided her with the "pros" and "cons" of medicine as well as with a significant amount of personal insight. The next thing we knew, Jamie had decided to take the MCAT test—the required exam for application to medical school. The exam was so grueling that she informed us by phone, "If God wants me in medical school, He needs to allow me to make a high enough score to be accepted, because I don't ever plan to take that exam again."

Apparently, God did want her there because Medical College of Georgia in Augusta (the very same hospital where Jonathan had undergone the week of intensive evaluation several years earlier) accepted her for the fall 1991 class.

Jonathan attended middle school for two years and then transferred to the local high school. He had done very well in middle school, but high school presented another big transition. There were so many students in the high school he would be attending. *What if he got lost? What if they ridiculed the special education students? What if? What if? What if?* My mind whirled constantly.

My prayer every time Jonathan had encountered new situations had always been that his teacher would love him and bring out the very best in him. I discovered before the school year began that his teacher would be a teacher who had previously taught at Rose Garden. Even though she had never taught Jonathan, she knew him well. Knowing that she had an excellent reputation, and she really loved her students helped ease my mind and supply much needed peace.

Chapter 35

"Pomp and Circumstance"

A ll my fears about Jonathan attending high school proved to be unfounded. Every day a team of "peer helpers" assisted in his class—different students each period—and they adopted Jonathan. They even included him in many of their activities, partially because he was the only verbal student in the special education class, but also because his social skills were his best asset. Almost every day they took him to the cafeteria for lunch and allowed him to eat with them at their table. They followed him through the food line, helped him select his lunch, and assisted him in getting his tray to the table without spilling anything. No small feat. They also had to be responsible for monitoring him and not allowing him to wander off. (Most of Jonathan's classmates ate lunch in the classroom because the teacher physically fed several students in his class.)

In October during his first year in high school, the entire student body named him "Student of the Week." The school boldly displayed his name in the cafeteria all week long for all to see. He loved it! Since he could read and spell his name, the peer helpers had to make numerous trips with him all week to the cafeteria so he could revel in his glory.

Towards the close of his first year in high school, he won two gold medals in swimming at Special Olympics state competition. Imagine his surprise when a message blared over the intercom at his school the following Monday morning congratulating him. He kept repeating over and over, "He said my name! He said my name!" It was almost as good as having his name displayed in the cafeteria.

A popular football player signed up to work as a student aide in Jonathan's class. On sunny days, he took Jonathan outdoors and pretended to play football with him. Sometimes they jogged around the track together. On rainy days, they challenged each other to a game of dominoes. Jonathan had no concept of the rules of dominoes, but he could count the dots and place matching dominoes side by side. The students allowed Jonathan to accompany them to school plays and Friday pep rallies. He would never master the complexities of the game of football, but no one could out-yell him at the pep rally. He proudly came home each Friday with game ribbons streaming down the front of his shirt.

His teacher recorded in his notebook: "Jonathan really has a fan club at Pope High School. He has students stopping by between classes every day just to say 'hello' to Jonathan."

We began to notice him speaking with more complete sentences and using an expanded vocabulary. Spending time with non-handicapped students was definitely having a positive effect on his ability to communicate. I was so proud of those students. It's easy for kids to ridicule and mock anyone who is different. However, those students showed an unusual level of maturity and unselfishness in their love and acceptance of Jonathan and his classmates.

The years had done nothing to squelch Jonathan's wandering spirit. He followed a pretty young student right into her art class one morning and sat down next to her. Instead of becoming irritated over the interruption, the art teacher seized the opportunity to talk to her class about the importance of looking out for the safety of the special education students and attempting to assist them if they needed help. Jonathan visited the drama class from time to time, and so as not to slight the sciences, he also wandered into the chemistry class occasionally. Even though there were over 2,000 students at his school, in no time at all, they all knew Jonathan well.

His tendency to wander landed him a spot in the time-out chair his second year of high school. His class had slowly trudged down the hall, headed to a school assembly. There were several wheelchair-bound students in his class, which made transporting the entire group from one location to another, a feat in itself. As they passed by the door leading outside where the school buses usually loaded and unloaded the students, Jonathan spotted a school bus with the door wide open. In retrospect, we could only surmise that he had thought it was his bus and it was time to go home. For whatever reason, he turned around unnoticed by his teachers, marched straight out the door, and climbed on the bus. Unfortunately for him, a group of math students headed for a field trip occupied that particular bus.

Not physically appearing handicapped can often be a handicap in itself. Because Jonathan looked like a normal student sitting on the bus, they were half-way to their destination before he opened his mouth and they realized "one of these kids is not like the others." As soon as the students made the bus driver aware of the situation, she turned the bus around and headed back to the school.

Of course, by that time his teacher had realized he was missing and had begun frantically searching the entire school for him. His reasoning ability is still almost non-existent to this day, so I'm sure he didn't have a clue what he did wrong. His teacher, understandably upset with him, made sure he kept the time-out chair warm for the rest of the day.

Jonathan's final high school psychological evaluation revealed the following:

His performance on intellectual testing yielded a mental age of four years and one month. The type of strengths and weaknesses that Jonathan exhibits are characteristic of a child who had developed a number of cognitive and verbal skills and then experienced brain damage. He has retained specific skills, but they are not entirely functional. His expressive language skills appear to be stronger than receptive language skills. He demonstrates strength in gross motor and fine motor skills, but a weakness in cognitive reasoning, language, and memory skills. Socialization is a definite strength for Jonathan. He responds positively to both familiar and unfamiliar people. His communication skills are particularly limited, however. He uses repetitive phrases and distorts words, and his sentence structure is often awkward and/or incorrect. He remains eligible for the Severely Intellectually Disabled program.

I had finally made peace with Jonathan's prognosis. For years, I had prayed, "Thy will be done," but I had obstinately refused to believe that God would not heal him mentally. I finally accepted the fact that God has a purpose for everything He allows. I could accept it and draw strength from it, or I could rail against it and wither spiritually. I needed His strength daily. God finally gave me the ability to accept Jonathan where he was, disabilities and all. Over the years, his progress had leveled out, so that even though he could learn new things on his level, he no longer progressed to higher levels. He would remain permanently disabled, unless God chose miraculously to intervene. And it was okay.

In 1995 we celebrated Jamie's graduation from medical school. She had chosen a specialty in pediatrics, and she planned to remain in Augusta and complete her residency at the Medical College of Georgia where she had attended medical school. We were thankful she would continue to be relatively close to home.

In 1998 we celebrated Jonathan's graduation from high school. A couple of weeks prior to the big event, we received a letter from Jonathan's school requesting our presence at an awards ceremony. I wrote his teacher a note and enclosed the letter we had received. "I feel sure this was sent to us by mistake, but just wanted to check," I wrote.

She responded, "No, it was not a mistake. Jonathan does need to be there along with you and Johnny. See you there." She offered no explanation. What a mystery. I couldn't begin to imagine why we needed to be at the awards ceremony.

We dressed Jonathan in his Sunday best and headed for his school on the designated evening. We met his teacher and found seats near the back of the room. We listened as the principal bestowed numerous awards and scholarships to deserving students. Then suddenly, the principal called Jonathan's name. His teacher grabbed his hand, and they slowly made their way to the front. The principal announced that Jonathan was receiving an award for all of his accomplishments in Special Olympics throughout his high school years. Jonathan accepted his award amidst thunderous applause from the audience. What a spectacular moment. Tears flowed unchecked down my cheeks as I reflected back on all the awards that Jamie had received over the years, never dreaming that we would ever attend an awards ceremony for Jonathan. God had surprised us with an unexpected graduation gift.

Jonathan took part in two graduation ceremonies. Traditionally, the special education teachers conducted a private graduation ceremony in the classroom for students, parents, and friends. Only four students were "graduating" and his teacher had planned a brief ceremony followed by a reception a few days before school ended. The school principal delivered a short speech and presented each graduate with a "diploma." Huge posters filled with photographs depicting special events in the lives of each graduate lined the room. The graduates' favorite snack foods were plentiful, along with a beautiful graduation cake.

We were happy Jonathan could celebrate with his special education classmates, but we really wanted him to be able to participate in the class graduation also. No student from the severely mentally disabled class had ever done that before, but we requested permission for Jonathan to walk across the stage and receive his diploma along with all his classmates. The school agreed.

My heart swelled with pride when I caught sight of Jonathan all dressed up in his cap and gown. He had never looked more handsome, and he really seemed proud of himself. He marched in with his teacher by his side as the familiar strains of "Pomp and Circumstance" played softly in the background. When the principal called his name, he and his teacher proceeded up the steps to receive his diploma. As he reached out to shake the principal's hand, his entire class rose to their feet in unison and filled the auditorium with ear-splitting applause—a standing ovation for our special little guy who had overcome so much in his life. I thought my heart might burst with joy.

No graduation would be complete without a post-graduation party, and Jonathan's would not be the exception. Linda and Jill, Jonathan's Sunday school teachers, threw themselves wholeheartedly into planning a huge celebration for him at a local restaurant. They reserved a private room and decorated it with balloons, streamers, and congratulatory signs in Jonathan's school colors. Presents covered a long table … a fitting end to a spectacular day.

Chapter 36

Watch for Flying Potatoes

Following his graduation from high school, we registered Jonathan for the county training center for the disabled. The training center offered day programs for the mentally disabled and job training for those who were capable of working. Unfortunately for us, in 1998 the state had slashed funding for the training centers to the point that services were limited, and waiting lists were growing longer by the day.

Jonathan name was added to a long waiting list with assurance that an opening should become available within six months. Six months came and went with no word of an opening. We continued to call, but always received discouraging news. No openings were available.

Jonathan became my shadow. Everywhere I went, Jonathan went also. When the women in our Sunday school class had a luncheon, Jonathan became our mascot. Every time I went shopping, he tagged along. Of course, all he wanted to do was ride the escalator.

On one occasion, my doctor sent me for a medical test that took several hours. Two of my close friends, Mary and Pam, had to accompany me and sit with Jonathan in the waiting room all morning.

By far, the most difficult situation, though, involved the bathroom dilemma. Because Jonathan lacked his entire colon, he had to make frequent trips to the bathroom. I obviously couldn't go in the men's bathroom, and since Jonathan still needed some assistance (not to mention that we couldn't trust him to come out), each time the urge hit him, I hauled him into the ladies' room with me. By that time, he was in his early twenties and had no distinguishing characteristics to identify him as handicapped. You get the picture.

Mary and Pam became my scouts. I would send them into the ladies' room to check out the situation. If they reported that the room was empty, I would quickly whisk Jonathan into the handicapped stall while my friends guarded the door. If I had no one with me, I had to pray we didn't terrify some unsuspecting lady. On more than one occasion, I witnessed women running from the room shouting, "There's a man in there!" It actually became humorous. I quickly became a real champion of places that had a "family" bathroom, a private facility intended for situations like ours as well as for nursing moms.

Speaking of humorous situations, one warm summer day Jonathan and I had returned home from running errands, after a final stop at the gas station to fill-up. When we returned home, I pulled into the driveway and stopped the car, intending to retrieve the mail before pulling into the garage. I left the car running, and as a safety precaution, I took Jonathan out of the car to walk with me the short distance to the mailbox. I've already mentioned that Jonathan is extremely obsessive/compulsive, and one of his obsessions involves locking the car doors. Before I realized what had happened, he had locked my door (which in turn automatically locked *all* the doors) and slammed the door shut. I quickly realized our dilemma: the car was running with a full tank of gas, my house keys and the garage door opener were both locked in the car, and Jonathan and I were left to bake in the hot summer sun.

I mentally scanned our situation. It was early afternoon, hours before Johnny would be home from work. It was also mid-summer and getting very hot. Jonathan tended to dehydrate very quickly in hot weather, which in turn triggered seizures. I knew I needed to get him out of the sun as soon as possible.

We walked to the next-door neighbor's house, and as luck would have it, no one answered the door. My parents had moved back to Alabama, and I didn't know the new neighbors who had purchased their house very well. I mentally berated myself for not giving someone in the neighborhood an extra key to our house. We trudged to the new neighbor's house, and thankfully, the husband had taken the day off from work and seemed eager to help. "If you don't mind, I'll just use your phone to call Johnny. He can come home from work with his set of keys and unlock the car," I said.

"No, no, no. There's no need to disturb Johnny at work. Let me think about this, and I'm sure we can get the car unlocked," my neighbor said. "Now, the first thing we need to do is stop the engine from running, or you'll waste an entire tank of gas. I'll be right back," he yelled over his shoulder as he hurried back to his house. He returned a few minutes later with a tennis ball. "Let's try putting this in the tail pipe to see if it will block the pipe and force the engine to stop."

"Okay, whatever you think," I said. That was definitely out of my league. The tennis ball, unfortunately, was too big for the pipe, but my neighbor was not the least bit discouraged. "Let me see what else I can find," he said. He obviously really loved a challenge. Back he came with a mysterious bag. "I have exactly what we need, a big bag of various sized potatoes. One of them should do the trick."

I stood back and observed, seriously beginning to question his mental state. The tail pipe was hot by that time, so he had also fetched a thick pair of gloves. On went the gloves, and in went the potato. Too small. He selected another. I made a mental note to purchase a bag of potatoes for his poor wife. Finally, he located just the right size. He shoved the potato into the tailpipe, pushing it in as far as possible. "It's a tight fit, but you need a tight fit to get the job done right." He made it sound as though he did that every day. "Now, any second the engine should cut off." He could hardly contain his excitement.

Suddenly, with the speed of lightning, the potato shot out of the tailpipe like a man flying out of a cannon! It flashed by us with such force I could only be thankful we weren't in its path. We think it landed somewhere in the neighbor's yard across the street, but truthfully, we never knew. No one ever saw that potato again. "Wow! That was amazing!" was his response. The engine was still running, the car was still locked, and the temperature outside was continuing to rise.

"I think I'll just go inside your house and call Johnny," I said with raised eyebrows.

"That's probably not a bad idea," he said in surrender.

After two long years of waiting for an opening for Jonathan at the local training center, we needed to pursue other options. We had lived in the same county for twenty-seven years and in our current house for about twenty-five years, but we began to explore programs for disabled adults in other counties. The first place we investigated was the county directly north of us. One Saturday we were driving around looking at different subdivisions when a real estate agent working in a subdivision we particularly liked began pressuring us to move.

"Our primary deciding factor when considering any move will be the programs available for our son," Johnny informed her, "and we have no idea at this point what this county has to offer." We thought that would get the eager beaver off our backs.

"I'll find out and let you know," she boldly declared.

We were astonished when she called us the following week with the location of the training center and the name of the person we needed to contact.

We visited the training center the following week. An employee gave us the grand tour and the paperwork to get the process started. We were extremely impressed with the program and the personnel. It seemed too good to be true. After two years of being on a waiting list, Jonathan would finally have a place to go each day where he could work on goals appropriate for him.

We went home and spent the next week praying about the decision. We both sensed God opening a door for us. We put our house up for sale the week following Christmas, and to our amazement, it sold in less than two weeks. Another confirming sign from God that we were on the right track.

Jonathan began attending the new training center in May 2000. We couldn't say enough positive things about his new center. The staff genuinely loved each person who attended.

A red-letter day occurred in our family February 17, 2001. We had prayed from the time of Jamie's birth that God would bring into her life exactly the man he had chosen as a mate for her. A mutual friend introduced her to Kevin at a singles' outing sponsored by her church. Kevin's infectious sense of humor proved to be a perfect balance for Jamie's more serious "doctor" personality. Kevin had the ability to create fun in any situation he encountered. Kevin proposed after several months of dating, and they set February 17, 2001 as their wedding date.

Jamie had always been adamant that whomever she married would have to love and accept Jonathan, disabilities and all. She had nothing to fear. Kevin quickly became the brother that Jonathan had never had. He teased Jonathan and pestered him, as any brother would, and Jonathan not only tolerated it, he actually seemed to enjoy it.

Jonathan's health had improved to the point that by 2003 he had succeeded in staying out of the hospital for over 15 years—remarkable for someone with his medical history. However, in September, 2003 a tragedy occurred.

Early one morning not long after he awakened, Jonathan headed for the stairs to look for me and Johnny. Normally, he races up and down the stairs with the agility of an athlete. I called for him to come to the bathroom for his shower while Johnny prepared to leave for work. Unfortunately, we didn't see what happened ... but we heard it ... a sickening sound. Thump, thump, thump, thump! We suspect that he had a seizure at the top of the stairs because he fell from top to bottom. Amazingly, he did not lose consciousness, and he didn't appear to be bleeding. However, lying at the bottom of the stairs, he moaned, obviously in excruciating pain. I immediately called Jamie, by now a practicing pediatrician who lived about an hour away. While Jamie and I were talking, Jonathan got up off the floor, walked to the family room, and laid down on the sofa.

"You need to call his doctor immediately, even if he seems okay," she said. "He has to be tested at the hospital to make sure nothing is broken." Good advice. After numerous x-rays, CAT, scans and MRI scans, we received the discouraging news. He had a burst fracture near the base of his spine. Simply put, his vertebra had burst, scattering fragments of bone. One of the bone fragments was pressing into his spinal cord. He also had a bone fracture higher up along the spine.

The hospital assigned Jonathan's case to an orthopedic surgeon who specialized in spinal injuries. We were grateful to learn that as a committed Christian, he had promised not only to do everything medically possible to restore Jonathan's broken spine, but also to pray for his complete recovery. "It is truly a miracle that Jonathan not only is alive after the fall he suffered, but that he is not paralyzed," he said.

We had two choices: Jonathan could wear a body cast for three months, or he could have spinal fusion surgery, which involved implanting titanium rods and screws all along the fractured areas of his spine. It was a no-brainer. He would never tolerate a body cast for three months. It would be torture for him and impossible for us to explain to him. The surgeon made an appointment with Jamie to discuss his options, the surgery, and the recovery process. She agreed with us that surgery was his best hope for recovery.

We assembled our prayer team and asked our church to put Jonathan's name on the prayer list. By the time the orderly rolled him into the operating room, a huge group of friends had assembled in the surgical waiting room. They came and went all day as the surgery stretched on and on. Finally, over six hours later, we got the long-awaited call from the surgical suite that it was over.

The surgery had successfully mended Jonathan's fragmented spine, but he spent almost a month in the hospital recuperating before he was able to come home. His quick recovery amazed even his surgeon. He returned to the training center after only three months. Today you would never be able to tell that he had undergone such extensive spinal surgery.

Jonathan celebrated his thirty-seventh birthday on January 11, 2013. He is happy and healthy and continues to live at home with us and attend the training center Monday through Friday. We may never know this side of heaven why Jonathan has had to experience so much pain, suffering, and loss in his short life. We do know beyond any shadow of a doubt, however, that God has a purpose for Jonathan. He has placed His healing hand on him time and time again. And in the process, God has taught us lesson after lesson about His abiding grace.

Chapter 37

Valuable Life Lessons

everal years ago, I read an essay by Emily Perl Kingsley, the mother of a child with Down syndrome, which succinctly described the road that we had walked with Jonathan. The essay is as follows:

"Welcome to Holland"
by
Emily Perl Kingsley

I am often asked to describe the experience of raising a child with a disability - to try to help people who have not shared that unique experience to understand it, to imagine how it would feel. It's like this ...

When you're going to have a baby, it's like planning a fabulous vacation trip - to Italy. You buy a bunch of guidebooks and make your wonderful plans. The Coliseum. The Michelangelo David. The gondolas in Venice. You may learn some handy phrases in Italian. It's all very exciting.

After months of eager anticipation, the day finally arrives. You pack your bags and off you go. Several hours later, the plane lands. The stewardess comes in and says, "Welcome to Holland."

"Holland?!?" you say. "What do you mean Holland?? I signed up for Italy! I'm supposed to be in Italy. All my life I've dreamed of going to Italy."

But there's been a change in the flight plan. They've landed in Holland and there you must stay.

The important thing is that they haven't taken you to a horrible, disgusting, filthy place, full of pestilence, famine and disease. It's just a different place.

So you must go out and buy new guidebooks. And you must learn a whole new language. And you will meet a whole new group of people you would never have met.

It's just a __different__ place. It's slower-paced than Italy, less flashy than Italy. But after you've been there for a while and you catch your breath, you look around ... and you begin to notice that Holland has windmills ... and Holland has tulips. Holland even has Rembrandts.

But everyone you know is busy coming and going from Italy ... and they're all bragging about what a wonderful time they had there. And for the rest of your life, you will say "Yes, that's where I was supposed to go. That's what I had planned."

And the pain of that will never, ever, ever, ever go away ... because the loss of that dream is a very, very significant loss.

But ... if you spend your life mourning the fact that you didn't get to Italy, you may never be free to enjoy the very special, the very lovely things ... about Holland.

Jonathan was not born disabled, neither does he have Down syndrome, but the lesson applies nonetheless. Perhaps it applies to your life as well. When any catastrophic, life-changing event takes place in our lives, we must choose whether we will spend the rest of our lives grieving over what we lost and what will never be, or thanking God daily for what we have learned along the way. The path that we choose will determine whether we grow and learn from the experience, or whether we live a life of misery and defeat.

A friend asked me recently, "What are the most valuable lessons God has taught you through your experience with Jonathan?" Her question prompted me to record some of them in hopes that others will benefit.

GOD ANSWERS PRAYER

Though He may not answer exactly as we would choose or in our timeframe, He always answers the prayers of His children. Jeremiah 33:3 says, "Call to Me, and I will answer you, and show you great and mighty things, which you do not know." "The Lord has heard my supplication; The Lord will receive my prayer" (Psalm 6:9). "In the day of my trouble I will call upon You, For You will answer me." (Psalm 86:7). "He hears the prayer of the righteous" (Proverbs 15:29b).

Even though God has performed many miracles in Jonathan's life, Jonathan remains severely mentally disabled with a very serious seizure disorder. For years I pleaded with God to restore Jonathan completely. When God failed to answer my prayers the way I wanted them answered, I redoubled my efforts. I spent hours on my knees trying to convince God that I knew best. When all my efforts failed, I became angry with God. "If you really loved me You would heal Jonathan completely," became a recurrent theme. Only when I surrendered my stubborn will to Him did I find His peace. When I began to pray, "Lord, if you choose to heal Jonathan, I will praise and glorify You. However, if You choose not to heal him, I will continue to praise and glorify You. Even if You choose to take Jonathan home to heaven, I will still praise and glorify Your name. Jonathan belongs to You, and You know better than I what is best for him and for us as well." I am convinced that until we are willing to surrender the circumstances of our lives completely to God, we cannot move forward spiritually.

God chose not to change Jonathan but to change me instead. My prayers changed from asking God to remove my pain to asking Him to teach me the lessons He wanted me to learn in the midst of my pain. Jonathan is very precious to us exactly the way he is, but more importantly, he is incredibly valuable to God, not because of what he will accomplish on this earth, but because he is a human being created by Almighty God in His image.

One of the most difficult, but valuable lessons, God taught me was that if I *only* love and trust God when He grants healing, I am worshipping the healing experience—not the Healer. Psalm 45:11b states, "Because He is your Lord, worship Him." We must worship Him not because of what He gives us or does for us, but because He is Jehovah God. Trusting Him means accepting His answer to our prayers whether it be "yes," "no," or "not right now."

GOD ALWAYS KNOWS WHAT IS BEST FOR US

It's easy to have faith in God and accept that He knows what is best for us when everything is going our way. When there's plenty of money in the bank, when everyone we know and love is healthy, when we're at the pinnacle of success in our career, God is so-o-o good. However, if we only love and obey God when everything in life is going our way, we're not learning to trust Him. We can totally place our trust in God; He has promised in His Word to provide strength and endurance for every situation we encounter. Trust doesn't mean trusting that God will give us everything we want—it means trusting that He will do what is best for us, regardless of what He gives or takes away. Often the things that appear tragic in our lives are the very things that God uses to mold us and make us more like Him. Habakkuk 3:17-18 states, "Though the fig tree may not blossom, nor fruit be on the vines; though the labor of the olive may fail, and the fields yield no food; though the flock be cut off from the fold, and there be no herd in the stalls— yet I will rejoice in the Lord, I will joy in the God of my salvation."

I personalized these verses with my own translation: Though Jonathan's thinking ability may never be normal, though his behavior may permanently remain like that of a three-year-old child, though Johnny and I may never experience the joy of loving a daughter-in-law, though we may be denied the treasure of being grandparents to Jonathan's children, yet we will rejoice in the Lord and joy in the God of our salvation.

My prayer is that my relationship to God will always be more important to me than a life void of problems. As long as I demand from God a life free from suffering, I will never grow spiritually.

WE CAN EXPERIENCE PEACE
IN THE MIDST OF THE STORM

Charles Spurgeon, a revered preacher from an earlier century, once said, "The promises of God shine brightest in the furnace of affliction, and it is in claiming those promises that we gain the victory." The darkest moments of our lives cause us to get very real about what we believe about God. I found myself often reexamining lessons I had learned in Sunday school as well as sermons I had heard over the years. Did I really, deep down, believe God's Word? Knowing that the answer was "yes" increased my faith and allowed me to move forward spiritually.

Whether or not we believe God's Word is reliable and His promises are true will determine our response to suffering, and our ability to experience God's peace.

We need to come before God daily and ask Him to reveal any area of our lives that is displeasing to Him. If He brings to mind sin that we need to confess, we can ask for His forgiveness; if He does not reveal any unconfessed sin, we can thank Him for His love for us and ask for His strength to meet the challenges we will face in the days ahead. Only then can we experience His cleansing and His power in our lives. Ask God for a teachable spirit so you can learn whatever lesson He may be trying to teach you in the circumstances you are going through.

While all of us hope for only good things to happen in our lives, that is not reality. Bad things do happen to all of us, and Christians are not exempt. Jesus said in Matthew 5:45b, "for He makes His sun rise on the evil and on the good, and sends rain on the just and on the unjust." In fact, we can experience pain and suffering even when we are being obedient. Jesus, Himself, experienced untold agony and suffering on the cross while being perfectly obedient to His father. Suffering gives us an opportunity to take the focus off ourselves and focus on Jesus. In the midst of the pain and difficulties we experienced with Jonathan, God definitely had my undivided attention. I desperately needed to hear from Him.

I'm convinced that there is no spiritual growth apart from suffering. I frequently hear people say, "If God really loved me, He would take away my pain, give me a successful job, solve all my problems ..." We must remember that God never promised us a comfortable life free from problems. In fact, He promised His followers exactly the opposite. Jesus told His disciples in John 16:33, "These things I have spoken to you, that in Me you may have peace. In the world you will have tribulation; but be of good cheer, I have overcome the world." He did promise to give us peace. Notice He said, "in me you will have peace"— regardless of sickness, loss of work, a failed marriage, even the death of a loved one. I can promise you from personal experience, you can find His peace in the midst of any tribulation.

GOD ALWAYS PROVIDES FOR HIS OWN

God has reinforced this lesson over and over, and He continues to provide for all our needs. When we experienced financial needs, He provided; when we needed friends to lift us up in prayer, He provided; when we needed help with meals and yard work, He provided; when we needed encouragement, He provided; when we needed someone to grieve with us, He provided. Over and over the Bible promises God's provision:

Matthew 6:8, 33: "…For your Father knows the things you have need of before you ask Him. But seek first the kingdom of God and His righteousness, and all these things shall be added to you."

Isaiah 58:11a: "The Lord will guide you continually, and satisfy your soul in drought."

Psalm 84:11c: "No good thing will He withhold from those who walk uprightly."

Psalm 37:4: "Delight yourself also in the Lord, and He shall give you the desires of your heart."

Psalm 34:10b: "Those who seek the Lord shall not lack any good thing."

Isaiah 43:1c-3a: "Fear not, for I have redeemed you; I have called you by your name; you are Mine. When you pass through the waters, I will be with you; and through the rivers, they shall not overflow you. When you walk through the fire, you shall not be burned, nor shall the flame scorch you. For I am the Lord your God,"

If we make ourselves available, God will use us to help meet the needs of those around us. God's Word commands us to bear one another's burdens. Galatians 6:2 instructs us to, "Bear one another's burdens, and so fulfill the law of Christ."

My friend, Gloria James, is a Bible study teacher, a counselor, and a precious friend and spiritual mentor. One evening I was so emotionally distraught over a situation concerning Jonathan I didn't realize the late hour and called her. I think I woke her from a sound sleep. She prayed with me over the phone and assured me of her continued prayers for Jonathan in the days to come. I thanked her and apologized profusely for calling so late. I have never forgotten her reply, "Louise, if something happens to a member of the body of Christ, it happens to all of us. If you are hurting, I am hurting with you." I Corinthians 12:26 states, "If one member suffers, all the members suffer with it; or if one member is honored, all the members rejoice with it." The Lord has used Gloria over and over to minister to the needs of others because of her availability.

GOD STILL PERFORMS MIRACLES

We have witnessed miracle after miracle and continue to see God's miracle-working power in Jonathan's life. I am amazed when I reflect back on all that Jonathan has been through in his short life, and yet he is healthy, happy, and content. We tend to think of miracles only in terms of life and death situations; however, God performs miracles all around us every day, though they often go unnoticed.

In 2004 one of our close friends, Mike Kelsey, began experiencing difficulty swallowing. His internal medicine doctor assured him it was probably nothing serious. However, just to be on the safe side, the doctor ordered a series of tests. I decided to meet Mike and his wife Pam at the clinic the day of the test, primarily to keep Pam, company during the long wait.

Mike and Pam had each come to a personal relationship with Christ as adults, and it had been a radical, life-changing decision. They joined the Sunday school class that my husband, Johnny, teaches, and we quickly became friends. We loved this couple as though they were physically part of our family. Johnny and Mike had been prayer partners for years, and Pam and I had as well.

It grieved us beyond words when Mike's doctor confirmed a diagnosis of advanced cancer of the esophagus—stage four. Shortly after receiving the news, Mike and Pam visited with us in our home. Mike knelt in the middle of our family room as the three of us laid our hands on him and pleaded with God to heal him of cancer. He then began extensive radiation and chemotherapy treatments.

Mike valiantly fought his disease for over three years, nevertheless, on February 3, 2008, his earthly battle ended, and God called him home.

Sylvia, another close friend of ours, developed colon cancer at the young age of forty-five. Her prognosis was not very encouraging, and our entire church, as well as others from around the world, prayed faithfully and earnestly on her behalf. We all believed with all our hearts that God would intervene and miraculously heal Sylvia. However, that was not the case. Sylvia went home to be with the Lord approximately two years after she received the diagnosis of cancer. I had an opportunity to visit with her the week before she died. Though she continued slipping in and out of consciousness, I held her hand and prayed with her for several hours. She only voiced one phrase the entire time I stayed with her. She repeated it over and over and over. "I want to go home; I want to go home; I want to go home." Sylvia had been at her earthly home for several months under the care of hospice volunteers, so I'm convinced in those last moments and days she had a glimpse of her heavenly home, and she longed to be there eternally.

On the other hand, doctors informed our pastor, Dr. Ernest Easley, in 1998 that he had a fast-growing malignant throat cancer. He endured forty-four radiation treatments that plunged his weight from 190 pounds to 144 pounds in a ten-week period. He relates in his book *Through the Valleys,* "As I entered the fifth week of treatment, I could no longer swallow because of the hundreds of ulcers on my tongue and throughout my mouth and throat due to the radiation. I was slowly dying of malnutrition."

Yet, God worked in a miraculous way to heal him completely of his disease. Dr. Easley has a powerful testimony, and God has used him repeatedly to lead many people to Christ and to minister to those who are hurting and suffering.

Why did God choose to heal our pastor and not Mike or Sylvia? They each had committed their lives to God and longed to serve

Him and glorify Him. I can't even begin to understand why many faithful Christians have prayed for healing and have instead died in the prime of life. Likewise, many who have prayed for healing have received a miracle from God and have gone on to live a long, full life. Isaiah 55:8-9 reveals, "For My thoughts are not your thoughts, nor are your ways My ways, says the Lord. For as the heavens are higher than the earth, so are My ways higher than your ways, and My thoughts than your thoughts." I do know if we belong to Christ, heaven is our ultimate home. Death for believers is not a punishment, it is our reward! I look forward to spending eternity in that glorious place.

We sometimes consciously or unconsciously say to God, "I really love the miracle that you performed in Tom's or Jane's life. Just give me the same miracle and I'll be happy." God, thankfully, does not work that way. He has a unique plan for each of our lives. We get very excited and joyful over reading about God's miracles of healing, and we should. However, we are often reluctant to read about the suffering and trials some of His followers endured, even though they had served Him faithfully.

We have to remember that everything we experience on this earth—whether joyful or painful—is temporary. (Even Lazarus, whom Jesus raised from the dead, eventually departed this earth, and everyone whom Jesus healed eventually died.) It is through the trials, tribulations, and suffering that we hear God speak the clearest. Philippians 3:10 states, "That I may know Him and the power of His resurrection, and the fellowship of His sufferings, being conformed to His death."

We all have many questions that God may not answer until we meet Him face to face. God has a purpose for everything He allows in our lives, though He may not always reveal it to us. One thing is certain: though God miraculously healed Dr. Easley, nevertheless, he will one day join Mike and Sylvia in heaven; and though God chose not to heal Mike and Sylvia on this earth, they would never change places with any of us after experiencing the joys of heaven. Though healing is wonderful, God never intended for us to worship the healing experience. Seeking miracles should not be our ultimate goal. When we belong to Christ, our purpose, whether we live or die, is to glorify God.

One of my favorite books of the Bible is Philippians. Paul wrote this book while a prisoner in chains and shackles. According to 2 Corinthians 11:24-27 Paul recorded, "Five times I received forty stripes minus one. Three times I was beaten with rods; once I was stoned; three times I was shipwrecked; a night and a day I have been in the deep; in journeys often, in perils of waters, in perils of robbers, in perils of my own countrymen, in perils of the Gentiles, in perils in the city, in perils in the wilderness, in perils in the sea, in perils among false brethren; in weariness and toil, in sleeplessness often, in hunger and thirst, in fastings often, in cold and nakedness."

What do you think Paul's reaction was to all these trials and afflictions? I know what mine would have been. Constant whining and complaining to God about the hand He had dealt me. Paul's attitude displayed none of that. In Philippians 3:8 he wrote, "I also count all things loss for the excellence of the knowledge of Christ Jesus my Lord, for whom I have suffered the loss of all things, and count them as rubbish that I may gain Christ."

Regardless of how much he had suffered, Paul considered it of no consequence—rubbish—in light of the fact that he belonged to Christ.

Chapter 38

A Life-Changing Decision

Considering all that Jonathan has experienced in his short life, I know that I would have lost all hope had it not been for a life-changing decision that I made at the age of eight. Even at that young age, I knew in my heart that Jesus Christ had died on a cross to pay the debt for my sin. The only way I could receive forgiveness for my sin and spend eternity with Him was to admit I had sinned, ask for His forgiveness, and turn my entire life over to Him. I walked down the aisle of a little church in Texas with my dad at my side and gave my life to Christ. My life has never been the same, and I've never regretted that decision for one minute. If you have never made this choice in life, I urge you do so today. Jesus Christ loves you more than you can comprehend and longs for a personal relationship with you. His plan of salvation is simple enough for a child to understand:

ADMIT YOU ARE A SINNER
Every person is in need of salvation.

"For all have sinned and fall short of the glory of God" (Romans 3:23).

Sin is committing any act that is displeasing to God and is in violation of His Word. Sin separates us from God. God is a just God and, therefore, must judge our sin.

"For the wages of sin is death, but the gift of God is eternal life in Christ Jesus our Lord" (Romans 6:23).

Since we are all guilty of sin, it is impossible for us to live a perfect life. The penalty for our sin is eternal separation from God in a place called hell. However, God is also a God of mercy and has provided a way for us to receive forgiveness of our sin and spend eternity with Him.

"But God demonstrates His own love toward us, in that while we were still sinners Christ died for us" (Romans 5:8).

Admitting that we have sinned and fallen short of God's plan for our lives and being willing to turn from our sins is the first step toward receiving God's gift of salvation.

BELIEVE IN JESUS
We cannot save ourselves.

"For by grace you have been saved through faith, and that not of yourselves, it is the gift of God, not of works, lest anyone should boast" (Ephesians 2:8-9).

Salvation is a gift from God to you. There is no way to receive salvation except through faith in Jesus Christ.

"I am the way, the truth, and the life. No one comes to the Father except through Me" (John 14:6).

Jesus is the only one who can save you.

"Nor is there salvation in any other, for there is no other name under heaven given among men by which we must be saved" (Acts 4:12).

Jesus' death on the cross and His resurrection from the grave provided the way of salvation for all who would turn from their sins and place their faith in Jesus.

"For God so loved the world that He gave His only begotten Son, that whoever believes in Him should not perish but have everlasting life" (John 3:16).

RECEIVE GOD'S GIFT OF SALVATION

God has provided the way for our salvation, but we must choose to receive His gift of eternal life. He created us with a free will and freedom of choice. Each person must decide for himself whether to accept or reject God's offer of salvation.

"I am the resurrection and the life. He who believes in Me, though he may die, he shall live. And whoever lives and believes in Me shall never die" (John 11:25-26).

Through prayer, invite Jesus to come into your life and take control. Confess your faith in Jesus Christ as your Lord and Savior.

"If you confess with your mouth the Lord Jesus and believe in your heart that God has raised Him from the dead, you will be saved" (Romans 10:9-10).

It's as simple as praying a prayer similar to the one below, but remember that there is nothing magical about the words. God's greatest desire is for you to turn away from your sins and willingly invite Him into your life to be your Savior.

Dear Lord Jesus,
I admit that I have sinned and need Your forgiveness. I want to turn from my sins and follow You. I ask You to forgive me of all my sins. I place my trust in You and You alone. I believe that You died on the cross and arose from the dead to pay the penalty for my sin. Right now I surrender my life to You. I invite You to come into my heart and life. I receive Your gift of eternal life and confess You as Lord and Savior of my life. Thank You for loving me enough to die for me. Thank You for giving me new life. Please help me live for You every day of my life from this day forward. In Jesus' name.
Amen.

GOD'S ASSURANCE
"Whoever calls upon the name of the Lord shall be saved" (Romans 10:13).

Romans 8:38-39 assures us that nothing can separate us from God's love, "For I am persuaded that neither death nor life, nor angels nor principalities nor powers, nor things present nor things to come, nor height nor depth, nor any other created thing, shall be able to separate us from the love of God which is in Christ Jesus our Lord."

"He who has the Son has life; he who does not have the Son of God does not have life. These things I have written to you who believe in the name of the Son of God, that you may know that you have eternal life" (I John 5:12-13).

You can be sure, if you sincerely prayed this prayer, God has saved you, and you now have eternal life; and abundant life.

"I have come that they may have life, and that they may have it more abundantly" (John 10:10b).

WHAT TO DO NEXT

As you begin your new life with Christ, learn as much as you can about Jesus. Read your Bible daily. The Bible is full of promises that God has made to you. God's Word provides the answer to every situation you will encounter in life.

Make prayer a daily habit. Prayer is simply talking with God. You can pray anytime about any situation. Find a church that honors Jesus Christ and teaches God's Word. Share your new commitment to Christ with as many people as possible. Jesus said in Matthew 10:32, "Whoever confesses Me before men, him I will also confess before My Father who is in heaven."

MY HOPE FOR YOU

Invariably, when Johnny and I meet people for the first time and they realize that we have a son who is severely mentally disabled, they are extremely sympathetic. They have no idea what a privilege it is for us to be Jonathan's parents. Unlike most of us, Jonathan is incapable of worry and is completely trusting of everyone. He never complains, gossips, criticizes, or judges others. God has given Jonathan the gift of joy, and he finds pleasure in the simplest things of life.

My prayer has always been that the things we have experienced with Jonathan and the lessons God has taught us would not be wasted. God did not make a mistake, nor was He looking the other way on January 9, 1983, when Jonathan had a stroke. Jonathan is incredibly valuable in God's sight exactly the way he is. The truth is, we are all valuable in God's sight, not because of our great intellect or contributions to society, but because God created each of us, and He loves us exactly the way we are.

Joel 2:25 reveals, "I will restore to you the years that the swarming locust has eaten." I believe with all my heart that one day we will see Jonathan in the morning—a bright, fresh new morning in heaven—and God will restore all the years that were lost on earth. I sincerely hope that Jonathan's story has strengthened your faith, encouraged your journey with God, or introduced you to new life in Christ. May God bless you abundantly.

Thank You For Reading This Book

It is my heartfelt desire that you have been drawn closer to God as you were reading this book. If you have been encouraged in your walk with God, have received Christ as your Savior, or would like to share with us how God has blessed you through this book please feel free to contact us via email at LouiseDFlanders@Bellsouth.net. We would love to hear from you.

TO ORDER ADDITIONAL COPIES

Go to WWW.AMAZON.COM or
other online stores

Then search on
**I'll See You in the Morning
by Louise D Flanders**